Teacher Quality, Teaching Quality, and School Improvement

Leslie S. Kaplan and
William A. Owings

PHI DELTA KAPPA
EDUCATIONAL FOUNDATION
Bloomington, Indiana
U.S.A.

Cover design by
Victoria Voelker

Library of Congress Control Number 2002111951
ISBN 0-87367-844-3

Table of Contents

DATE DUE

GAYLORD			PRINTED IN U.S.A.

Introduction

In the summer of 1998, nearly 60% of Massachusetts' aspiring teachers failed an exam that state officials described as a test of eighth- to 10th-grade skills (Fowler 2001). This disturbing but misleading fact, widely discussed on op-ed pages across the country, highlights the national concern about the quality of teachers and teaching. As Minner said, "Teacher quality is not just an important issue in addressing the many challenges facing the nation's schools: It is *the* issue" (2001, p. 33).

Improving the quality of teachers and teaching has become the "third wave" of education reform (Hirsch et al. 1998, p. 2). Education policy makers have spent years trying to reform schools by imposing increased graduation requirements, tougher standards, and high-stakes testing on students. However, unless changes occur inside the classroom with improved teaching and learning, our goals for preparing students for self-sufficiency in the 21st century will fail. Better teaching is the key to higher student achievement. If teachers do not know enough, students cannot learn enough. Thus 49 states have set standards for teachers with high-stakes assessments, and the No Child Left Behind legislation requires these assessments to begin in 2005-2006 for reading and math in all 50 states.

We know what constitutes good teaching, and we know that good teaching can matter more than students' family backgrounds and economic status. There is significant research to indicate it is the quality of the teacher and teaching that are the most powerful predictors of student success. The emerging data strongly assert that students with three consecutive years with effective teachers (as compared with ineffective teachers) can make students' achievement appear as if the students are gifted (Sanders and Rivers 1996). Moreover, Haycock (1998) writes that we can close the "achievement gap" between affluent white students and poor and minority students if principals assigned the best teachers to students who most need them.

Ironically, at the very time that schools face increased public and professional pressures for student achievement, education faces a critical teacher shortage. Schools in the United States will need to hire 200,000 K-12 teachers annually for the next 10 years to meet increasing student enrollments and teacher retirements (Resta, Huling, and Rainwater 2001). High teacher turnover rates complicate the shortage problem (Ingersoll 2002). Experts estimate that 30% to 50% of all new teachers will leave the profession in their first five years. Thus, for the foreseeable future, schools will face the multiple challenges of recruiting and keeping effective teachers while strengthening the teaching skills of those already in the classrooms.

This book shows principals, superintendents, and other instructional leaders how to increase student achievement by hiring high-quality teachers and supporting their professional practice. It presents research showing how high-quality teachers affect student achievement and explains why teachers and teaching quality matter if schools are to teach all children to high levels. The first part discusses issues that affect teacher quality, including strong content knowledge, teacher licensing and certification practices, and recruitment and retention concerns. The second part carefully reviews how teachers' best instructional practices affect student achievement, essential factors in teaching for learning, what quality teaching "looks like" in action, the effect of class size, and how effective professional development strengthens best practices. It also considers how equity and high-stakes testing relate to teaching quality.

Hiring and keeping high-quality teachers while actively supporting enhanced teaching quality in each classroom are the true keys to higher student achievement.

Why Quality Matters

What teachers bring to the schoolhouse matters. For years, educators debated which factors influenced student achievement. Early research suggested that schools have only a limited effect on achievement. Researchers argued that a student's family and social background played the major roles in setting learning limits (Coleman et al. 1966, p. 325). However, more recent data suggest that teacher qualifications play a significant role in how much students learn (Ferguson 1991; Darling-Hammond 2000; Haycock 1998, 2000; Wenglinsky 2000).

In a 50-state survey, Darling-Hammond (2000) found that while such student demographics as poverty, minority status, and language background are strongly related to student outcomes in reading and math at the state level, these factors appear less important in predicting individual achievement levels than do "teacher quality" variables, such as holding full certification and a major in the field. Moreover, teacher preparation has a stronger connection with student achievement than do class size, overall spending, or teacher salaries (Darling-Hammond 2000, p. 33). According to Darling-Hammond, teacher preparation accounts for 40% to 60% of the total variance in student achievement after taking into account the students' demographics (p. 27).

The 50-state survey found that the following teacher quality factors are related to increased student achievement:

- Verbal ability.
- Content knowledge.

- Education coursework on teaching methods in their discipline.
- Scores on state licensing exams that measure both basic skills and teaching knowledge.
- Teaching behaviors, including purposefully, diagnostically, and skillfully using a broad repertoire of approaches.
- Ongoing voluntary professional learning.
- Enthusiasm for learning.
- Flexibility, creativity, and adaptability.
- Teaching experience (teachers with less than three years classroom practice are less effective, but there is little difference among teachers with more than three years of experience).
- Asking higher-order questions and probing student responses.
- Class sizes, planning time, opportunities to work with colleagues, and curricular resources.

The qualities that teachers bring to the classroom make a measurable difference in how well and how much students learn. Educators need to take careful note of these factors when hiring teachers. By doing so, they invest in their students' future achievement.

In this book, we use the terms "teacher quality" and "teaching quality" to mean different things. "Teacher quality" includes the *inputs* that teachers bring to the school, including their demographics, aptitudes, professional preparation, college majors, teacher examination scores, teacher licensure and certification, and prior professional experiences. "Teaching quality" refers to what teachers *do* with what they know to promote student learning *inside* the classroom. "Teaching quality" includes creating a positive learning climate, selecting appropriate instructional goals and assessments, using the curriculum effectively, and employing varied instructional behaviors that help all students learn to high levels.

Both central office and site-based leaders play major roles in ensuring teacher and teaching quality in their classrooms.

Understanding the research on teacher and teaching quality can help school policy makers, principals, and key instructional leaders significantly improve student achievement.

What teachers do in their classrooms affects student achievement for better or worse. This is not a new idea. As Haycock writes, "Parents have always known that it matters a great deal which teachers their children get" (1998, p. 3). Haycock quotes Eric Hanushek, a University of Rochester economist: "The difference between a good and a bad teacher can be a full level of achievement in a single school year" (p. 3). Research confirms that teachers' classroom expertise — teaching quality — is an essential factor in student achievement (Darling-Hammond 1999; Haycock 1998, 2000; Hill and Crevola 1999; Sanders and Rivers 1996).

A study by ETS examined the math and science scores of nearly 15,000 eighth-graders on the National Assessment of Educational Progress in 1996 (Blair 2000; Wenglinsky 2000). When their teachers had strong content knowledge and had learned to work with children from different cultures or with special needs, the students tested more than one full grade level above their peers. Similarly, when teachers integrated hands-on learning and frequent in-class teacher assessments into their lessons, the students tested 72% ahead of their peers in math and 40% ahead in science. Students whose math teachers stressed critical thinking skills, such as writing about math, scored 39% higher than did students whose teachers did not stress those skills. In addition, "the aspects of teaching quality measured (in this study) have an impact seven to 10 times as great as that of class size" in affecting student achievement (Wenglinsky 2000, p. 31). Unfortunately, the report notes, too few teachers use the practices associated with higher scores.

A value-added study in Dallas estimated that the average reading scores of fourth-graders assigned for three consecutive years to highly effective teachers rose from the 59th percentile in fourth grade to the 76th percentile by the sixth grade. Comparable reading scores of other fourth-graders assigned to three years of ineffective teachers were at the 60th percentile in fourth grade but had fallen to the 42nd percentile by the end of sixth grade. This reflects more than 35 percentile points difference for students who started at approximately the same level (Jordan, Mendro, and Weerasinghe 1997). Similarly, third-graders with comparable math scores at the 55th percentile rose to 76th percentile by the end of fifth grade after three consecutive years with highly effective teachers while peers with three years of the least effective teachers scored at the 27th percentile by the end of fifth grade. This 49-point difference in three years is particularly noteworthy as schools prepare to meet adequate yearly progress requirements of the No Child Left Behind (NCLB) legislation (Jordan, Mendro, and Weerasinghe 1997).

A Tennessee value-added study found similar results. Fifth-graders scored at the 83rd percentile in mathematics after three consecutive years of very effective teachers, while students who had ineffective teachers scored in the 29th percentile (Sanders and Rivers 1996), a difference of more than 50 percentile points. The most effective teachers produced gains of 53 percentile points for low-achieving students during one school year.

Dramatic differences in student achievement gains appear for low-, middle-, and high-achieving groups of students (Haycock 1998). In one year, high-achieving students gained an average of only two percentile points under the least effective teachers but averaged a gain of 25 percentile points under the most effective ones. Middle-achievers gained only 10 points under the least effective teachers but gained more than 30 points with the most effective teachers.

High school students also show achievement gains from quality teaching. In 1998, Boston 10th-graders who were working with teachers rated in the top third quality continuum had average achievement gains that exceeded the national median. Students with those teachers ranked in the lowest third showed virtually no growth in achievement. Both student groups started the year with similar math and reading scores. Their only educational difference was teaching quality (Haycock 1998).

Furthermore, data from the 1998 National Assessment of Educational Progress indicate that effective teaching makes a difference in minority student achievement. On the eighth-grade writing test, average scores for African-American students ranged from 121 points in Arkansas to 146 points in Texas, a 25-point difference worth about 2½ years of learning. In addition, on the same eighth-grade writing test, Latino scores ranged from 106 in Mississippi to 146 in Virginia, equivalent to three to four years difference in learning (Haycock, Jerald, and Huang 2001). Both Texas and Virginia were among the first states to implement high-stakes testing. These strong results for minority students may reflect the increased emphasis on teaching quality to bring all students to higher standards. In fact, these teacher-dependent differences in achievement within minority populations are greater than the learning gap between whites and minorities in most states (Haycock, Jerald, and Huang 2001).

These studies strongly suggest that students with effective teachers make significant achievement gains, while students with less effective teachers may actually lose ground. The investigations also point to troubling indicators for both educational equity and achievement. Low-income and minority students are nearly twice as likely as others to be assigned to the most ineffective teachers and only half as likely to be assigned to the most effective teachers (Haycock 2000; Hirsch, Koppich, and Knapp 1998; Jordan, Mendro, and Weerasinghe 1997; Reeves 2000; Sanders and Rivers 1996). Some data indicate that poor African-American students are less likely to have a well-qualified teacher than are poor white students (Kain and Singleton 1996).

In short, teacher and teaching quality — what teachers *do* with what they *know* in their classrooms — make important differences in how much — or even whether — students learn. Over time, students with a series of effective teachers learn successfully and advance to challenging courses and continued education. Their peers achieved just as well a few years earlier; but without the cumulative benefit from effective teachers, students later performed poorly on standardized tests. Over time, their lower achievement in school and on gatekeeping tests and courses restricts their opportunities for further education, higher achievement, and challenging careers. Differences in teacher and teaching quality have life-altering consequences for students and ultimately for society.

Educators who want high-quality choices for all students must look more closely at the diverse factors contributing to teacher and teaching quality and make informed decisions about whom to hire and how to keep them. Reviewing the research connecting teacher inputs with student achievement offers a clear starting point for such decisions.

Teacher Quality

Teacher quality refers to the inputs teachers bring to the classroom. Decisions about teacher quality involve content knowledge, licensure, and certification. Each state sets its own cutoff scores on state licensure tests to decide how much content knowledge teachers need to be employed in the state. Within the past few years, more than 25 states enacted legislation to improve teacher quality through recruitment, education, certification, or professional development (Darling-Hammond 1997). The No Child Left Behind Act offers additional definitions of "highly qualified" teachers for states' considerations.

Content Knowledge

When teachers have college majors or minors in the subjects they teach — especially in secondary math and science — their students outperform students whose teachers do not have this strong content knowledge (Blair 2000; Goldhaber and Brewer 1999; Haycock 1998, 2000; Wenglinsky 2000). The 1996 NAEP data (Blair 2000; Wenglinsky 2000) of eighth-graders' performance on math and science finds that students whose teachers majored or minored in those subjects outperform their peers by about 40% of a grade level (Wenglinsky 2000). Other evidence suggests that teacher content knowledge in English and social studies may be no less important (Haycock 1998).

No evidence suggests that, by itself, possessing content knowledge is enough to be an effective teacher (Berry 2001). Some claim that the connection between teachers' subject knowledge and student achievement is mixed, positively influencing student learning up to a certain level of basic competence but less important after that (Darling-Hammond 2000; Monk 1994). In fact, studies show that knowledge both of subject matter and of teaching and learning are strongly correlated with teachers' classroom performance (Guyton and Farokhi 1987). Teacher education coursework is sometimes more influential than extra subject matter coursework in promoting students' math and science achievement (Monk and King 1994). Others add that college majors vary in rigor, and a prospective teacher's college transcript may not actually confirm teacher knowledge (Kanstoroom and Finn 1999). Similarly, Education Trust examined state licensure exams and stated, "Most of the context on licensing exams is most typically found in high school curricula . . . never at the level of a bachelor's degree" (Mitchell and Barth 1999, p.15).

While strong content knowledge has a demonstrated link to higher student achievement, it may be a necessary but not sufficient condition for quality teaching. However, Haycock asserts that content knowledge — not necessarily "education courses completed, advanced education degrees, scores on professional knowledge sections of licensure exams nor . . . years of experience" (1998, p. 3) — has a clear relationship to student achievement.

Licensure and Certification

Licensure and certification are the state's formal approval of teaching candidates for professional practice. For many purposes, the terms are used interchangeably. They serve as professional benchmarks for teacher quality and reflect strongly on teacher preparation programs.

If all students are to be held to high standards, then teachers must be held to high standards. Because teacher content knowledge is a recognized factor in student achievement, ensuring that teachers meet high standards means "guaranteeing" they have the subject knowledge and professional skills essential for high-quality teaching. Awarding teacher licensure or certification is the state's way of verifying a minimum level of teacher competence, and a passing score on a licensure test is frequently one of the state's requirements for initial teacher certification.

Testing fitness to teach has a long history in the United States. In 1686, Virginia's legislature asked the governor to name examiners for schoolmasters in every county (Levinson 2001). The recent push to measure teacher competence began in the 1970s. Currently, every state now requires that public school teachers hold a certificate or license, similar to those required for physicians and lawyers. In all but six states, teachers must pass one or more written, standardized tests measuring basic literacy and math, knowledge of teaching methods, and specialty subjects. These six hold-out states (Idaho, Iowa, South Dakota, Utah, Washington, and Wyoming) use other means to assess teacher competence and skills. States set the passing scores and usually permit those who fail to retake the tests until they pass (Levinson 2001).

The No Child Left Behind Act of 2001 requires all core academic teachers to be fully certified by the 2005-2006 school year. Teachers hired after fall 2002 without full certification violate the legislation.

In addition to the "quality control" function of protecting the public by licensing only competent educators, teacher-licensing is also big business. During the 2000-2001 school year, approximately 500,000 prospective teachers took ETS tests and 377,000 took National Evaluation System (NES) tests. One official estimate is that teacher testing for certification generates $50 million to $100 million or more each year for testing companies (Levinson 2001).

Several teacher tests currently are used to determine competence for licensure. The Educational Testing Service's (ETS) Praxis II test is an exam that measures teacher's content mastery. The NES is a private test-making company that contracts with 10 states (California, Texas, New York, Illinois, Michigan, Massachusetts, Arizona, Colorado, Oklahoma, and New Mexico) for custom-made tests. The state-designed Massachusetts Educator Certification Tests (MECT) consist of two, separate, four-hour exams including subject matter, reading, and writing. These formal tests are intended as an entry standard for new graduates of teaching programs, as well as for beginning teachers coming from other routes.

The proportion of teachers in a state who have full certification and a major in the field they teach is the most significant predictor of student achievement in reading and math. The proportion of new teachers who are uncertified usually predicts the lack of student achievement (Darling-Hammond 2000). Hiring fully qualified teachers is advantageous when schools want to raise student achievement. One study of more than 1,000 school districts concludes that every additional dollar spent on more highly qualified teachers nets greater improvements in student achievement than does any other expenditure (Ferguson 1991).

Although critics say teacher licensing exams are not rigorous, not all classroom teachers pass Praxis II, NES, or MECT on the first try. Before NCLB, they could teach with a temporary license until they passed, which could be several years later, depending on their state requirements. In times of teacher shortages in certain subjects, passing a standardized test becomes an additional hurdle to placing teachers in every classroom. When states faced teacher shortages, failing the test usually did not prevent a candidate from being employed, though such positions often were temporary. North Carolina, for example, gave new teachers additional time — two years instead of one — to pass the Praxis II (Silberman 2001a).

Unfortunately, the high failure rates of prospective teachers on licensure tests may reflect poorly on college teacher preparation programs. Schools of education receive public criticism for accepting students unable to successfully complete college work. Commentators censure many candidates' low academic quality. Faced with possible "decertification" if too few of their graduates pass licensing tests, some schools of education require prospective teachers to pass all certification tests before entering student teaching, thus "shifting the burden of program accountability . . . to the backs of the students" (Fowler 2001, p. 779).

> The question is whether the means that policy makers are using to improve schools of education — more certification tests, higher cut scores, and severe penalties for schools that fail to meet specific pass rates — will deliver the increased accountability and better teachers that policy makers have demanded. (Fowler 2001, p. 779)

Teacher quality is no longer an accountability issue only for schools of education and preservice teachers. Some states are planning to administer competency tests to veteran educators to ensure they have mastered their subjects. Facing crises in math education and public confidence, the Massachusetts State Board of Education adopted the "first in the nation" required testing of veteran middle and high school math teachers in "low performing" districts. In these schools, more than 30% of the students — not counting the non-English speakers (LEP) and new arrivals — failed the MCAS math section. The board wanted to assure themselves and the public that teachers really knew the subjects they were teaching. Teachers associations argued against the "test the teacher" regulations and took their fight to court. The court rejected their claims (Hayward 2001). One teachers union official noted, "Passing a test makes it harder to attract and retain qualified teachers when there's a teacher shortage looming" (Vaishnav 2001, p. 3).

Licensing standards may not guarantee teacher quality because they may not require teachers to have enough content knowledge to help all students learn to high levels (Mitchell and Barth 1999; Ballou and Podgursky 1997, 1999). For example, while 44 states require candidates for secondary licenses to take some kind of licensing exam, only 29 require them to take tests in the subjects they will teach (Mitchell and Barth 1999). In addition, licensure requirements tend to emphasize more pedagogical than content knowledge (Mitchell and Barth 1999), and teacher content knowledge is the key factor in student achievement. Moreover, certification tests do not measure teacher's verbal ability, another known predictor of classroom effectiveness (Fowler 2001; Cobb et al. 1999).

While paper-and-pencil licensure tests are not irrelevant to teaching quality, they do not correlate well enough with teacher quality to serve as the primary means to ensure it (Fowler 2001; Madaus and Pullin 1987). Some argue that the time-consuming and costly teacher preparation activities required for teacher licensure actually may prevent content experts from entering the classroom (Kanstoroom and Finn 1999; Ballou and Podgursky 1997; Lederhouse 2001). Disagreement also exists about whether any teacher exam "cut-score" should bar "otherwise qualified" individuals from becoming teachers (Ballou and Podgursky 1999).

What does matter is the amount of content knowledge teachers have. Superintendents and principals need some way to ascertain this critical information about a candidate's academic expertise. Haycock explained, "While subject-specific teaching certificates and college majors don't tell you everything about content knowledge, they are at least a reasonable proxy" (2000, p. 4).

Teacher Preparation Accrediting Programs

Receiving an endorsement from a public or private accrediting body is one way in which teacher education programs show their worth. Several organizations grant independent accreditation of teacher preparation programs through a formal review and evaluation process that holds schools of education to certain standards.

The National Council for Accreditation of Teacher Education (NCATE) is a coalition of 33 professional organizations representing different segments of the education community. NCATE member organizations include the American Federation of Teachers, the National Education Association, the Council of Chief State School Officers, the National School Boards Association, and several national "specialized professional associations." NCATE currently accredits 525 of the nation's 1,200 teacher-preparation programs. Forty-six states evaluate teacher-preparation programs using NCATE standards or benchmarks closely aligned with them, and 28 of these states require all teacher-preparation programs to earn NCATE accreditation (Blair 2001*c*).

In 1954, NCATE started to professionalize teaching with the first written national standards for the teaching profession, articulating what it believed are the necessary features of high-quality teacher preparation programs and the knowledge and skills their graduates should have when starting classroom practice. Before this, individual states and regional accrediting bodies or teachers college groups accredited teacher preparation programs, each creating its own evaluation model. Such haphazard practices lacked both the public and professional appearances of accountability (Blair 2001c). NCATE, on the other hand, became a way to assure the public that a program was one of high quality.

NCATE evaluates an institution's ability to meet six standards, including the program's evaluation system, courses offered, field and clinical experiences, performance and development, leadership, and resources. Accreditation also includes determining such factors as number of volumes in the school library and the number of faculty publishing articles. NCATE looks for diversity within the prospective teaching corps, the faculty, and the children served. Moreover, since 2001, NCATE has started using a performance-based accreditation system that looks more closely at the quality of the candidates' work, subject knowledge, and demonstrated teaching skills, rather than primarily monitoring inputs and processes not directly connected to classroom practice (NCATE 2000).

NCATE membership costs between $1,600 and $3,000 annually, depending on the size of the education department or school. An accreditation evaluation costs approximately $10,000 to $12,000. In addition, some departments have to spend money to bring their programs up to NCATE standards (Blair 2001c).

Before NCATE implemented its 2001 performance standards, critics noted that NCATE did not look at the quality of a program's graduates, focused too heavily on methods courses at the expense of solid college majors in content areas, and was too detailed and prescriptive. They added that the accreditation process had extremely high costs in money and person-hours. NCATE, they further claimed, also neglected to fully disclose evaluation information to the institution to use for constructive feedback. Moreover, the diversity component made it difficult for many smaller colleges, which do not attract African-American or Hispanic teacher-educators, to meet this NCATE criterion (Blair 2001c).

Data are mixed on whether NCATE-trained teachers are superior to those from non-NCATE endorsed teacher education programs. A study by the Educational Testing Service (ETS) in 1995-1997 on the qualifications of 270,000 candidates found that individuals from NCATE-accredited institutions passed Praxis II licensing exams at a higher rate (91%) than did those from unaccredited institutions (84%) or those with no teacher preparation (74%) (Wise 2001, p. 3).

On the other hand, two surveys from the U.S. Department of Education observe that on most measures, little difference exists between the NCATE and non-NCATE groups (Ballou and Podgursky 1997, p. 22). Likewise, no difference appears in their professional commitment. More than half of both groups intend to spend their entire careers as teachers. More than 80% of both groups find teaching positions. Finally, 80% of both groups say they would choose to become teachers if they had to choose again (Ballou and Podgursky 1997, p. 22).

NCATE and non-NCATE groups differ, however, with respect to race and ethnicity. While NCATE schools supply only 41% of all teachers, these schools supply 52% of minority teachers and 65% of Hispanic teachers (Ballou and Podgursky 1997, p. 22). Their graduates tend to work in inner cities, teach in schools with large numbers of minority students, and are more likely to have limited-English-speaking students in their classrooms. They also are likely to be trained to work with such students.

Although NCATE requires a teacher education program to screen applicants for admission, their criteria for test scores are vague, as are their criteria for "successful completion" of the program. In addition, the academic abilities of a program's graduates has little effect on determining whether the program will be accredited. Small liberal arts colleges and the more selective universities are less likely than larger colleges to seek NCATE approval (Ballou and Podgursky 1997). In fact, only 20% of teachers from NCATE-accredited institutions are from highly competitive colleges that accept 15% or fewer of their applicants (Ballou and Podgursky 1997, p. 24).

To date, NCATE-accredited programs cannot claim superiority in teacher quality over non-NCATE-accredited programs.

The Teacher Education Accreditation Council (TEAC) is a new accreditation body that allows teacher education programs seeking approval from an outside agency to set their own standards. This alternative to NCATE has been endorsed as a national accreditation body by the Council for Higher Education Accreditation, a Washington-based watchdog group (Blair 2001c). The National Association of State Universities and Land-Grant Colleges, the American Association of State Colleges and Universities, and the National Association of Independent Colleges all endorse TEAC. Although not approved by the U.S. Department of Education, some consider TEAC worthy of providing rigorous evaluations of collegiate academic programs.

TEAC grew out of the quality movement in business and industry. TEAC claims that NCATE's academic benchmarks and other requirements are not validated by research and concludes that the benchmarks represent nothing more than its founders' subjective consensus. The TEAC Board of Directors includes college presidents, teacher-preparation administrators, and a classroom teacher. TEAC provides a framework within which colleges and universities can set their own benchmarks for judging their teacher-preparation programs, thus encouraging self-reflection. However, no teacher-preparation program can set low standards, because TEAC requires proof that the institution is doing an effective job preparing teachers.

Programs seeking TEAC accreditation provide auditors with students' grades, scores on standardized entrance and exit exams, surveys of graduates' employers, portfolio assessments by faculty members, and information about such related activities as tutoring children and participating in community services. Faculty members use multiple measures to outline compliance.

Unlike NCATE, TEAC accredits individual teacher-preparation programs, rather than entire schools of education, education departments, or institutions. A two-person auditing team performs an external evaluation using data and interviews to determine that the schools' programs meet their own goals as well as TEAC's three basic quality principles. Those principles are: 1) students must master both subject-matter content and pedagogy, 2) the program has a valid assessment to measure learning, and 3) the school must use its self-evaluation to continuously improve its program (Blair 2001c). Accredited programs also must meet standards for regional accreditation and state approval, institutional standards for academic degrees, and other relevant state licensure criteria.

Proponents argue that TEAC's accreditation process allows schools to set higher standards than those set by other accrediting agencies. However, critics argue that TEAC is a weak accountability model because the schools set their own standards, rather than seek to reach those set by outside experts with broader expectations. TEAC allows colleges to secure national credentials while avoiding their responsibilities to meet clearly defined standards (Blair 2001c). The critics argue that the lack of clear, rigorous, national standards inhibits the professionalization of teaching. Meeting a widely recognized benchmark, they add, is particularly important in a mobile society.

Accrediting teacher-preparation programs may be an important factor in ensuring quality teachers. However, currently there is no empirical evidence that supports one accrediting body over another.

Alternative Teacher Certification

The need for teachers is growing. Student enrollments continue to rise while thousands of educators leave the profession each year. This has forced education leaders to consider alternative certification. Strong alternative certification routes can help candidates find jobs, school districts fill vacancies, and policy makers gain appealing options to traditional teacher education.

Alternative certification programs bypass traditional teacher education timeframes, course contents, and clinical learning experiences, often placing new teachers into classrooms prior to certification. About 250 institutions now offer alternative routes to teacher certification for people who have had careers or baccalaureate degrees in subjects other than education (Basinger 2000).

The number of teachers entering the profession through alternative avenues is increasing. "Researchers estimate that 80,000 teachers have entered teaching by a nontraditional route over the past decade" (Berry 2001, p. 33). In 1998-1999, more than 24,000 teachers received certification through alternative routes in the 28 states that keep these data. Forty-one states now have alternative certification programs, removing the need for prospective teachers to return to college for an education major before entering K-12 classrooms. Two-thirds of the colleges and universities preparing teachers have at least one graduate program for mid-career professionals (Berry 2001). Alternative programs also are attracting a more diverse teaching force (Berry 2001; Finn and Madigan 2001).

Alternative certification programs vary in content, duration, rigor, and support for learning how to teach. They range from graduate-level programs to short-term programs with reduced licensure requirements to "traditional emergency hiring practices that fill vacancies by letting virtually anyone teach" (Berry 2001, p. 33).

Alternative certification programs are not all equal. Their expectations and quality vary greatly, and the implications for student learning are profound. Accordingly, administrators must look carefully at their teaching applicants' specific alternative certification programs to ensure that they are hiring teachers who can help all students learn to high levels.

"Shortcut" certification programs give teacher candidates four to eight weeks of training in classroom management, developing lesson plans, and related material and then place them in classrooms as fully independent teachers, with minimal supervision and often with the most disadvantaged learners. The new teachers take education courses at night and on weekends, and the courses often are not connected to their classroom practices. They work without trained mentors on the job or in their training programs. In addition, because there are no specifications for what these teacher candidates should know, certification programs have varying expectations for "classroom readiness" (Berry 2001).

High-quality alternative teacher preparation programs include:

- Sufficient time, generally from nine to 15 months, and professional learning experiences before entering the classroom as an independent teacher.
- Strong academic and pedagogical coursework.
- Intensive field experience with internships or student teaching under the direct daily supervision of an expert teacher.
- The expectation that new teachers meet all the state's teacher-quality standards.
- The expectation that new teachers gain full state teacher certification within a specified time (Tell 2001; Berry 2001; Darling-Hammond 2001).

The research is ambiguous on how well these new teachers perform. Some evidence suggests that alternatively certified teachers cannot handle the job (Berry 2001; Darling-Hammond 2001). Studies find that recruits who have bachelor's degrees and who completed short-term alternative certification programs, but who have not completed full teacher certification requirements, tend to have difficulty with curriculum development, teaching methods, classroom management, and student motivation (Berry 2001; Feiman-Nemser and Parker 1990). Berry (2001) adds that alternatively certified teachers also have more problems with organizing and sequencing lessons, responding to students' learning needs, and encouraging higher-level thinking. In one study, principals rated alternatively certified candidates significantly lower than those prepared traditionally on instructional skills and instructional planning (Jelmberg 1996). It appears that some alternatively certified teachers may know their subject, but not in ways that help them organize or present it for student learning.

Other studies (Goldhaber and Brewer 1999) cautiously state that no significant differences in teacher effectiveness exist between those with emergency certification and those with standard certification, as long as the teachers have majors in the content taught. Using National Educational Longitudinal Study (NELS) surveys of 24,000 students surveyed in 1988 and again in tenth (1990) and 12th (1992) grades, researchers used various factors to explain students' scores on standardized math and science tests. NELS ties detailed teacher and class information directly to individual students. The researchers speculate that the school districts that employed teachers with nonstandard certification might have screened them for thorough knowledge of content, and they suggest readers interpret their findings cautiously. They add that little rigorous evidence exists that relates teacher certification to student achievement.

In addition, brief certification programs do not produce a stable, high-quality teaching force. A recent analysis notes that 60% of individuals who enter teaching through "shortcut programs" leave the profession by their third year, compared to 30% of traditionally trained teachers and only 10% to 15% of teachers prepared in five-year teacher preparation programs (Berry 2001, p. 34). On the other hand, students in the traditional four- and five-year programs may have a very different commitment to teaching as a lifetime career than do teachers in "short-cut" options (Ballou and Podgursky 1997). The first group deliberately seeks and prepares for a chosen career. The second group may want only to "try it out" before making a final decision. Persistence — or lack of it — in the classroom may reflect these other factors as much as it does the education components of their professional training.

Several noteworthy alternative certification programs exist. Such programs include Teach for America, Troops to Teachers, Massachusetts Institute for New Teachers, and the Delta Secondary Teacher Education Program. Moreover, many colleges and universities, either alone or in partnership with K-12 school systems, offer other certification programs.

Teach for America. Since 1990, Teach for America (TFA) — now part of Americorps Service Program — has recruited, trained, and placed more than 800 recent college graduates each year in low-income U.S. schools (Ness 2001). TFA recruits bright but inexperienced college graduates with a strong social commitment, leadership skills, and initiative to see if they like teaching. At the same time, it provides children in poverty with well-educated, motivated teachers and role models. Participants make a two-year commitment to the schools in which they are placed.

The training is not extensive. Prospective teachers first conduct independent classroom observations and reflect on what they see. They bring their reflections to a five-week summer institute, where they learn theories of education, holding children to high expectations, lesson planning, student assessment, and working with low-income communities. TFA then places its teachers into schools with other TFA teachers and alumni and with principals and teachers who support them. Novice teachers observe and meet with high-performing teachers to learn best practices. Participating in regional and interregional meetings, receiving newsletters, and accessing the Teach for America website also give support. Likewise, partnerships with local universities encourage new teachers to continue their formal education and to work toward licensure (Tell 2001). Many complete their state credentialing during their two years of service (Ness 2001).

Critics note that TFA teachers do not receive adequate training and that a two-year commitment is not enough time to make meaningful changes in already challenged schools (Tell 2001). TFA responds that 60% of TFA alumni are still in education, and at least 40% are now principals and assistant principals. TFA does not address the quality of their teaching or the degree of their students' learning.

Troops to Teachers and Military Transition Programs. Troops to Teachers (TTT) is a federally funded program that provides referral assistance and placement services to military personnel interested in beginning second careers as public school teachers. TTT has approximately 3,500 participants in training programs in 47 states, and 2,900 of their new teachers have been hired by schools. Twenty states operate Troops to Teachers Placement Assistance Offices. All military personnel, including Coast Guard and veterans, are eligible if they have at least a bachelor's degree from an accredited college. Those without a bachelor's degree can be considered for teaching vocational or technical subjects but must be able to document their skill level or expertise. However, some state offices ask for an associate degree as a minimum entry requirement.

Old Dominion University (ODU) in Norfolk, Virginia, boasts one of the first Military Career Transition Programs (MCTP) affiliated with Troops to Teachers. Started in 1989, the program provides a streamlined route to teacher certification for active duty and former military personnel. While program entry requires an associate's degree, more than 90% of enrolled students have a bachelor's degree and 40% have a master's degree (Basinger 2000).

MCTP students must complete 30 credit hours, including a minimum of six weeks of student teaching, and usually can earn certification and a master's degree within 18 months. Courses are offered off-campus and during evenings and weekends to accommodate mature students still working in the military, allowing them to move into teaching without having to take time off and lose income. Veteran schoolteachers and administrators teach all the courses as adjunct instructors, connecting master teachers with adult learners who respect practical expertise. The MCTP currently enrolls approximately 1,300 students. More than 1,250 military officers and senior enlisted personnel have been certified as teachers through this program and now work in 47 states. Since the program's inception in 1989, 95% of the graduates have become teachers, and 90% remain in the profession (Basinger 2000).

The TTT certification program emphasizes practical training and depends on developing collaborative relationships with schools. This allows teaching candidates to infuse pedagogical coursework with field-based experiences while working with mentor teachers in schools. Troops complete one year of coursework before taking their six weeks of student teaching. During their first semester, however, they take a practicum in which they spend time observing and working in schools. They also take an introductory course in classroom management, designed to help them evaluate themselves and make the transition — in job and in personal identity — from the military to teaching. In addition to coursework and certification, this transition program also provides counseling and advising, training program referrals, employment links, and career induction assistance.

The Massachusetts Institute for New Teachers. Using the Teach for America model, the Massachusetts program recruits teachers to work in high-need schools for a $20,000 signing bonus. A seven-week summer training program includes 100 hours of student teaching and coursework on classroom management, pedagogy, and education theory. Candidates who successfully complete the course receive a state license (Tell 2001).

One-fifth of these new teachers leave the classroom after one year, citing insufficient mentoring or administrator support (Viadero 2001). Regardless of teaching quality or high turnover, the signing bonus continues to attract candidates; and sites were expanding for the 2001-2002 school year (Tell 2001).

The Delta Secondary Teacher Education Program. Affiliated with the George Washington University School of Education in Arlington, Virginia, this program offers a master's degree in secondary education and a teacher license to transitioning professionals from diverse careers (Tell 2001). This is a flexible, self-paced curriculum for prospective teachers who remain employed through most of their training. It usually lasts from 16 months for teaching licensure to two or three years for the master's degree. Participants complete coursework and 60 hours of observations at school sites before starting a semester-long, full-time internship.

How effective are alternative teacher certification programs? Programs that insist on strong content knowledge and provide rigorous and sufficient pedagogical coursework integrated with supervised field experiences can bring enthusiastic, able, and often certified new teachers into classrooms. Furthermore, onsite expert support during the induction period, ongoing professional development, and clear expectations for meeting the state's teacher quality standards within a limited time help keep these new teachers in the classroom, helping students learn.

Teaching Out of Field

By itself, teacher certification does not ensure high-quality teachers. One widespread practice that lowers teacher quality is to assign "otherwise qualified" teachers to classes in which they lack minimal academic credentials. "Requiring teachers to teach classes for which they have not been trained or educated harms teachers and students" (Ingersoll 2001, p. 42).

One-third of all secondary school math teachers have neither a major nor a minor in math or in such related disciplines as physics, engineering, or math education. Nearly one-quarter of all secondary school English teachers lack majors or minors in English, literature, communications, speech, English education, or reading education. More than half of the secondary school students enrolled in chemistry, physics, earth science, and space science are trying to learn from teachers who did not major or minor in any physical science. The situation for social science and social studies teachers is worse (Ingersoll 2001).

Out-of-field teaching varies across schools, teachers, and classrooms. Recently hired teachers are more often assigned to teach subjects out of their field than are more experienced teachers, and low-income public schools have more out-of-field teachers than do affluent schools. Similarly, smaller schools, junior high and middle schools, and lower-achieving classes are more likely to have out-of-field teachers (Ingersoll 2001).

Disagreement exists about the percent of "out-of-field" teachers. Traditional teacher education associations apply one set of definitions and cite a certain set of data based on these terms. Those who challenge traditional preparation programs sometimes use different definitions and advance other statistics. Moreover, not all colleges require students to declare formal academic "minors," even though students may take many courses in a desired concentration but fewer than qualify as a "major." For example, depending on the point of view to be advanced, either more than half (Ingersoll 2001) or only 14% (Ballou and Podgursky 1997) of high school students taking physical science have teachers who lack a certificate and a degree or minor in one of the physical sciences. Such differences in data and interpretation hold true for all teaching areas.

Of course, different writers may have their own objectives to advance. Accordingly, they propose solutions to support their beliefs, such as requiring more formal academic coursework or increasing the use of alternative certification. Readers need to be cautious and to note the specific meanings and contexts for data presented by these writers.

The national movement to increase teacher entry criteria and to enact tougher teacher certification requirements will not end out-of-field teaching assignments if central office staff and principals continue to assign teachers to subjects for which they are not certified. This lack of fit between a teacher's training and classroom assignment turns qualified teachers into unqualified teachers, resulting in lower student achievement and increased teacher frustration.

Recruitment and Retention Issues

One common complaint is that a teacher shortage keeps schools from hiring high-quality teachers. However, Darling-Hammond notes that the number of new teachers prepared annually — roughly 190,000 — is more than enough to satisfy the demand. Instead, schools face shortages of people certified in such subjects as math, physical science, special education, and bilingual education, especially qualified teachers who are willing to work for the salaries and under the conditions offered in specific locations. Moreover, Ingersoll's study points to a "revolving door" that increases teacher turnover from job dissatisfaction, pursuit of other jobs, and migration to other schools, rather than teachers leaving their classrooms for retirement. Special education, math, and science are especially vulnerable to high turnover rates (2002, p. 17). While some states have shortfalls, others have a surplus of applicants. Wealthier districts tend to have surpluses; poorer districts have shortages. Growing districts need more teachers than do those with declining enrollments. For some districts, cumbersome hiring practices discourage teacher applicants from applying and often result in late hiring and less-qualified applicants. Moreover, 30% to 50% of new teachers leave within five years, with a higher attrition rate in disadvantaged districts (Darling-Hammond 2001).

Finding and keeping quality teachers is a continuous challenge. A number of state and local policies affect these tasks, including recruitment, salary, incentives, career ladders, and equity.

Salary: "The teacher shortage plaguing school districts nationwide will not abate unless salaries improve," American Federation of Teachers President Sandra Feldman was quoted in a 17 May 2001 Associated Press report. While higher salaries are not the only way to recruit and retain teachers, they do make a difference.

Sadly, reports from the two national teachers unions suggest that educators are losing ground over time, a problem that increases the difficulty of attracting quality teachers (Archer et al. 2001). While teachers' salaries have risen slightly in the past several years, they have not kept up with inflation. The average salary for teachers rose 3% in the 1999-2000 school year, while the total personal income in the U.S. during the same period increased 5.9%. Measured in constant dollars, teachers' average salaries grew less than 1% between 1989 and 1999. Ten years ago, U.S. teachers' salaries were 21% higher than those of the average full-time worker. By the 1999-2000 school year, that figure had fallen to 10% (Archer et al. 2001). Modest salaries make attracting high-quality educators difficult.

Starting teacher salaries also fell further behind those of other white-collar professions. Teachers in their twenties can expect to earn about $8,000 less per year than other college-educated professionals, and the gap widens to $24,000 for persons age 44 to 55. For those with a master's degree, the gap climbs to $32,000 (Chase 2000). Specifically, while a new teacher could expect to earn about $27,989, college graduates could expect an average starting salary of $47,112 for engineering, $46,495 for computer science jobs, and $40,242 for business positions (Associated Press 2001).

In addition, traditional teacher compensation plans pay for seniority, rather than performance. The number of years teaching and bonuses for advanced formal coursework determine a teacher's or administrator's salary. This practice discourages high-achieving professionals from entering a career where only longevity, rather than productivity, will be rewarded.

Enticing beginning teachers with high initial salaries is one approach some districts use to attract high-quality teachers. A Houston area school district, for example, boasts the highest local starting teacher salary, at $35,000 (Markley 2001). New York City raised its starting salary from $31,910 to $39,000 in 2002 (Goodnough 2002).

Instead of a salary scale that pays teachers for seniority, school districts need to consider designing innovative compensation schemes to pay more for teachers with knowledge in shortage fields, for teachers who are more effective in increasing student achievement, for teachers who accept instructional leadership roles, and for hard-to-staff schools. Many potential high-quality teachers want careers where their salary will keep pace with their performance (Finn and Madigan 2001). As more schools provide a "pay for performance" option, additional well-educated individuals, as well as high-performing teachers, will find professional teaching an attractive career option.

Pay-for-Performance: Increasingly, states and localities are starting to experiment with salary structures as they try to recruit and retain high-quality teachers. In 2001 Iowa lawmakers replaced their traditional teacher compensation system with one that includes paying educators for performance in the classroom and students' achievement. They wanted to recruit promising young teachers to the state and retain veterans by rewarding their hard work with better pay and opportunities to quickly advance their careers (Blair 2001*a*). All Iowa school districts are required to participate by July 2003.

This $40 million package, believed to be the first in the United States, would allocate $2,000 cash rewards for teachers and others employed in schools whose pupils showed improvement on assessments. It was piloted in six schools in fall 2001. Local districts define what constitutes improvement and decide which measures to use to gauge gains. Once implemented, the new plan allows teachers to advance within the revised salary schedule at their own pace, with talented educators eligible to earn the top pay within five years, rather than gradually advance one year at a time.

Pay-for-performance is attracting national interest but little action. The Nebraska Legislature discussed a teacher pay-for-performance plan in 2001 but decided that "it was too bold." New Mexico passed a pay-for-performance bill, but the governor vetoed it; and Ohio lawmakers discussed a pilot project but failed to pass the bill (Okamoto 2001). Douglas County, Colorado, and Cincinnati schools also have pay-for-performance programs (Blair 2001*b*).

Concerns about pay-for-performance include finding enough funds to pay for all eligible educators who want to compete for them, locating enough qualified administrators to conduct needed teacher evaluations, designing ways for teachers to contest unfavorable evaluations, and deciding how to phase in the plan so that all qualified teachers might participate.

Many experienced teachers and teacher associations express serious reservations about pay-for-performance. They prefer the "neutral" salary practices that reward such inputs as teacher seniority, courses taken, and additional degrees earned, rather than rewarding such measurable accomplishments as higher student achievement. Competing for bonus dollars or earning salary increases, they allege, reduces collaboration and collegiality, both of which harm the learning climate and student achievement.

Career Ladders and Leadership Roles: "Teaching remains one of the few professions where novices have the same responsibilities as 25-year veterans" (Keiffer-Barone and Ware 2001, p. 56). This poses problems for prospective and beginning teachers who feel overwhelmed. It also tempts experienced teachers who seek broader professional responsibilities and higher salaries to leave their classrooms for administrative or non-teaching positions (National Commission on Teaching and America's Future 1996).

Career ladders support teacher advancement through ongoing professional development and creative compensation structures. In the Cincinnati Public Schools, for example, the career ladder includes the following steps: internship, apprentice, novice, career, advanced, and accomplished, with each step requiring increasingly higher quality teaching performance (Danielson 1996; Keiffer-Barone and Ware 2001). Classroom performance that affects students' learning, rather than teacher seniority, determines movement up the career ladder.

The Cincinnati Public Schools have a successful career ladder program that begins during the start of teacher education, the second year of college. Working with the University of Cincinnati and the Cincinnati Federation of Teachers, the public schools collaborated to design a five-year program with two degrees, one in the teacher's content discipline and a second in education. The program also includes a full-year internship that combines half-time teaching with university study and Professional Practice Schools, where both university and public school faculty mentor interns. Interns work with mentor teachers in city schools, observing classrooms and tutoring students. In their fourth year, they student teach. In their fifth year, they receive salary as half-time intern teachers with the support of university and public school mentors. Outstanding performers receive early teaching contracts in March. Second-career candidates with bachelor's degrees can complete the program in two years, and teaching aides are encouraged to complete certification (Keiffer-Barone and Ware 2001).

In Cincinnati's Career-in-Teaching program, each teacher level has a defined set of professional responsibilities and a base pay with additional salary for completing advanced degrees and earning additional certifications. Interns receive part-time pay as they meet university requirements for coursework and performance. Apprentices are first-year full-time teachers, and they are expected to earn a "basic" or better rating on numerous performance areas or domains (on a four-point rubric: Unsatisfactory, Basic, Proficient, and Distinguished) to qualify to be "novices." Novices take courses in such topics as classroom management, cooperative learning, standards for student learning, and developmentally appropriate practices, with salary increases for successfully completing these courses.

Teachers may choose to be evaluated in their third, fourth, or fifth years to determine their level of teaching. "On the basis of this evaluation, novices can move to the *career* level, and outstanding performers may jump directly to the *advanced* or *accomplished* categories" (Kieffer-Barone and Ware 2001, p. 58, emphasis in original). To reach the career level, teachers must receive "proficient" or better in all assessed domains. Advanced teachers need "distinguished" ratings in the Teaching for Learning domain and one other domain and "proficient" in the other two domains. Accomplished teachers need a "distinguished" rating in all domains.

The results of this program are encouraging. Ohio districts hire 85% of the teachers trained in this program, as compared to 45% of other newly certified teachers in the state. "Career-in-Teaching" teachers also receive higher evaluations than do other new teachers (Keiffer-Barone and Ware 2001). In addition, over the past five years Cincinnati's attrition rate has been less than 10% per year, lower than the national average (Fideler and Haselkorn 1999). This plan rewards teachers financially for the knowledge and skills they demonstrate at any point in their careers and also provides incentive pay increases above base salary. With this compensation model, high-performers have varied professional incentives to remain in teaching and to improve their teaching quality.

Many school districts provide master teachers with roles and responsibilities for professional development and teacher observation, coaching, and evaluation. For example, 99.6% of the teachers who have earned their National Board Certification have been offered invitations to become leaders and serve as professional coaches in their schools (Archer 2001c). These teachers usually train other teachers on instructional best practices, evaluate and assist new teachers, or help other teachers who are seeking National Board Certification (Archer 2001c). Frequently there are salary supplements for these leadership responsibilities.

Florida, Illinois, Massachusetts, and New York State pay master teachers to act as mentors to other educators (Archer 2001c). In Montgomery County, Maryland, each school has its own staff development teacher working full time to raise the school's overall instructional level. These teachers serve as instructional coaches, working with colleagues in small groups or individually to help improve classroom instruction and student achievement. They also help colleagues develop professional growth plans for continuous improvement. In addition, Montgomery County's new job-review procedures involve master teachers in decisions about which colleagues are competent and which should leave teaching.

In Rochester, New York, master teachers instruct students during part of the school day and participate in division leadership activities for the rest of the day. Master teachers in Seattle also have input into whom their school hires (Archer 2001b).

Unfortunately, not all teacher leadership opportunities have happy endings. Kentucky's Highly Skilled Educators Program invested $35.2 million over 11 years to train outstanding teachers to consult for two to three years in poorly performing schools and promised these teachers that, after their consulting term ended, they would have positions that used their expertise in their home districts. However, a majority of the 110 consultants from 1994-2000 did not find appropriate positions back home. While 48 returned to their former school districts, only 33% of them reported using their new skills. Twenty-five percent left public schools to become private consultants, and 10% left Kentucky to work in another state (Blair 2001*a*). Many schools lacked funds or personnel policies to support these instructional leadership positions. However, some critics suggested that principals were unwilling to accept a school culture of teacher leadership. In 2001 Kentucky policy makers were considering both offering bonuses to school districts to support salaries for these consultants and developing an alternative certification program for former consultants who want to become principals (Blair 2001*a*).

Instructional leadership positions open opportunities for skillful and ambitious teachers' professional advancement while continuing to affect classroom practices. Teacher leadership creates attractive career options for talented instructors who wish to advance professionally because it provides financial rewards and maintains their focus on enhancing teaching quality.

Other Incentives: While competitive salaries, generous benefits, pay-for-performance, and career ladders lure many teachers to certain localities, other schools extend different incentives to sign new teachers. Some school districts are offering such monetary incentives as relocation costs; signing bonuses for teachers in hard-to-fill areas, including math, science, special education, and bilingual education; and increased salary schedules that pay higher wages for new teachers. One school district gives $5,000 bonuses for certain subjects, signing bonuses paid over two years with an extra $1,500 given during the third and fourth years to reduce the expected 40% turnover at that time, and another $500 if the candidate had a 3.0 grade-point average or better in college (Markley 2001).

When it comes to finding new teachers, a few localities are "growing their own." For example, in May 2001 Palm Beach County, Florida, signed contracts with 39 graduating high school students, each of whom was promised a teaching job with the district after completing college. The jobs depend on students maintaining a 2.5 or higher college grade point average, passing a background check, and completing requirements for a state teacher's license. All the students participated in the "teacher academy" at their high school, a four-year program that gives students college-level courses on teaching, in addition to firsthand experiences (Archer 2001*a*).

Recruiting "Second Career" Teachers

Career switchers have become essential to fully staffing school faculties. For example, in North Carolina more than 800 of the state's 82,000 public school teachers in the 2000-2001 school year worked under emergency one-year permits granted to people who lack certification and a college degree in the subjects they were teaching. These career-switchers filled more than 4,300 classroom jobs — nearly 44% more than two years earlier (Silberman 2001*b*).

Mid-career adults bring maturity, life experience, and good work habits, along with a depth and breadth of content knowledge. They know how their subject is used in the "real world." In addition, teachers who enter the field at an older age have lower attrition rates than do those who enter at a younger age (Grissmer 2000).

These second-career adults are assertive and determined, with little patience for bureaucratic procedures and paperwork that they believe interferes with their work with students. They expect teaching colleagues and administrators to work collaboratively in solving problems, providing constructive criticism, mentoring and moral support, in-class assistance, and peer coaching. They also expect support in difficult situations (Resta, Huling, and Rainwater 2001).

Substantial federal and state resources are focused on recruiting and preparing teachers. Since 1999 the Title II Teacher Quality Enhancement Program has awarded $98 million to 32 state departments of education, 33 partnerships involving teacher preparation institutions, and 27 individual teacher recruitment projects to support efforts to increase the supply and quality of teachers (U.S. Department of Education 2000).

To meet this need, there are increasing numbers of lateral-entry teacher preparation programs. These are intensive, flexible, accelerated, field-based programs that allow mature participants who are already college graduates to earn initial certification before employment as teachers. For example, Troops to Teachers is a lateral-entry teacher preparation program. While some of these programs are brief but intensive (Silberman 2001*a*), many lateral-entry teaching programs have:

- Strong content preparation aligned with state and national standards.
- Rigorous curricula in pedagogy, including human growth and development, principles of teaching and learning, classroom management, instructional strategies, assessment of student learning, curriculum development and integration, technology applications, and content teaching.
- Substantial amounts of structured fieldwork and intensive clinical experiences.
- Support from peers and mentors throughout the induction period (Resta, Huling, and Rainwater 2001, p. 62).

The Teacher Recruitment and Induction Project (TRIP): Designed specifically for mid-career adults, this federally funded, collaborative program involving the Southwest Texas State University College of Education, Science, and Liberal Arts and seven school districts provides an alternative path into teaching. It recruits talented persons holding bachelor's degrees and provides an intensive program of integrated content, pedagogy, and technology that allows them to complete initial certification requirements in one year or less before they are employed as teachers. During their first semester, students combine a full schedule of 15 credit hours with two days a week observing, tutoring, and teaching students at a high-needs elementary or secondary school. Professors model instructional best practices as they integrate instruction and assignments with students' classroom experiences and provide immediate feedback on teaching practices. Participants complete student teaching during their second semester and take a graduate course one afternoon per week. Full-time mentors provide weekly support during their two-year induction into the profession (Resta, Huling, and Rainwater 2001).

NC Teach: North Carolina offers summer programs for lateral-entry teaching candidates on several of its university campuses. They provide intensive, five-week training programs before candidates enter the classroom as teachers. Prospective teachers take classes in child development, teaching strategies, psychology, and "public school culture," including understanding education jargon. The program also includes additional coursework in the fall and spring and a network of support as new teachers begin employment (Silberman 2001*b*).

Lateral entry teachers need up-front, focused, and ongoing education, as well as collegial support, if they are to help students learn and feel satisfied about their professional effectiveness. To be successful, they need the same preparation as other teachers need — strong curriculum knowledge, understanding of diversity, and a repertoire of varied instructional strategies. Without these, they soon leave the classroom in frustration. The national attrition rate for lateral-entry teachers runs as high as three times that of traditionally certified teachers (Silberman 2001*b*).

Recruiting Minority Teachers

Requiring prospective educators to meet stricter standards for content knowledge and certification sometimes appears to conflict with the goal of providing students with a diverse teaching corps. While minorities constitute 40% of U.S. public school students, only about 13.5% of public school teachers have minority backgrounds, according to the National Center for Education Statistics (Reid 2001). And according to Jorgenson, "The proportion of teachers of color are shrinking and fewer culturally diverse students are entering the profession" (2001, p. 64).

The political dichotomy between equity and quality is a red herring and reflects its own prejudice. While providing U.S. classrooms with a diverse teacher corps has substantial merit for many reasons, ensuring that all teachers are capable of teaching students to high levels is a goal that will raise all students' achievement. Both equity and excellence must be goals for recruiting and hiring teachers.

There are a variety of strategies to increase the pool of talented minority educators, such as recruiting at colleges with large numbers of ethnic students, including minority professionals on recruiting teams, and ensuring that recruiters have an understanding of cross-cultural issues. Human resource personnel also can use nontraditional networks for recruiting minority teachers, such as sororities and fraternities, campus organizations, the armed forces, community groups, and churches (Jorgenson 2001). School districts can work closely with local two- and four-year colleges to attract talented minority undergraduates into the teaching profession. And schools can collaborate closely with their communities to bring well-educated immigrants into teacher preparation programs (Ross 2001). One useful strategy is to solicit feedback from minorities on the strengths of a school and where it needs to be improved, especially on those aspects of the school that are important for recruiting and keeping minority employees.

Since 1990, Phillips Academy in Andover, Massachusetts, has sponsored the Institute for Recruitment of Teachers, which has helped 364 African Americans, Hispanics, and Native Americans to complete master's and doctoral degrees in education. The institute helps students apply to graduate education schools, matches applicants with universities, and prepares students for rigorous advanced studies during a month-long summer program. Students of color who cannot attend the institute receive counseling through the graduate process by telephone, fax, and e-mail. Phillips Andover's institute is privately funded and its services are free. Of those students helped by the institute, almost one-third are working in elementary and secondary schools and 149 have received or are working on their doctorates (Reid 2001).

Enhancing Teaching Quality

Teacher quality is what teachers know and bring to the classroom. *Teaching quality*, however, is what teachers *do* with what they know once they get inside the classroom. It includes the strategies and techniques teachers use to get students to learn.

Education leaders can help improve teaching quality by providing their teachers with strategies to increase their effectiveness in the classroom. These strategies include understanding and applying the evidence on how students learn, using instructional best practices, enhancing strategies for instructional observation and evaluation, providing effective and ongoing professional development, and establishing a common vision for philosophical beliefs about students and teaching.

Essential Elements of Quality Teaching

There are many variables that affect instruction, including the subject, grade level, learners' needs, and desired outcomes. Even the best teaching techniques require variety if they are to keep students' interest and enthusiasm for learning. Teachers who do not use a repertoire of effective instructional strategies "have limited images of good teaching" (Wasley 1999, p. 9).

While teachers need strong content knowledge in the subjects they teach, content knowledge is not enough to ensure that students learn. Recent research stresses that teachers must know the learning needs of each of their students. Students are not empty receptors into which teachers pour information. Instead, students mediate learning through their personal experiences, interests, prior knowledge, learning styles, and thinking. High-quality teaching deliberately uses these dimensions in the learning process. As a result, teaching for meaning and recall requires very different plans, strategies, and time frames than those used when teaching for superficial content coverage.

Connecting Learning to What Students Already Know. Teachers need to help students integrate new information with their existing beliefs. They need to regularly assess students' current understanding of a subject so that they can correct errors in students' knowledge and expand the correct ideas that students have.

New learning must be explicitly connected to the content that each student already understands and uses. Teachers also must help students understand when, why, and how new facts are relevant in their lives. Only when students have time to find or create sense and personal meaning out of the new information can they achieve a deep understanding that transforms facts into usable knowledge. This need to find meaning is important not only for high-achieving students who are comfortable with abstract concepts. It also is essential for low-achieving students, who require personal meaning *before* they can master a topic (Knapp, Shields, and Turnbull 1995).

Varied Instructional Repertoires. Learners vary in the ways they take in and master information. Thus teachers need to use a range of effective instructional practices that connect to students' favored learning approaches. No one strategy works well for all content, at all times, or for all learners.

High-quality strategies require providing learning experiences through a variety of physical senses to increase the likelihood that students will remember and later retrieve this information. The more senses a teacher involves in the lessons, the richer the students' capacity to recall information. Instructional strategies that employ students' senses include: expressing concepts verbally and visually (graphic organizers, peer teaching, summarizing, role playing, paraphrasing); moving (field trips, rearranging classrooms); employing routine and practice (flash cards, repetition, music); and experiencing positive emotions around important ideas, facts, and skills (music, debate, role playing, drama). All these approaches increase student engagement, retention, and recall of information and skills (Sprenger 1999).

Assessments Monitor Individual Progress and Guide Instruction. Assessment is an integral component of teaching and learning. Effective teachers monitor every student's progress daily and provide specific feedback to reinforce or correct each student's thinking. Students' oral and written responses to questions, their comments during small-group discussions, and their nonverbal expressions of understanding or confusion give teachers data about students' mastery of a subject.

Effective teachers also help students understand how to monitor and assess their own progress with such approaches as taking notes, planning ahead for projects, using flash cards, and monitoring their own learning.

Assessments should provide additional learning opportunities for students. Well-developed rubrics, for example, offer clear models for producing high-quality student work. Assessments that apply knowledge and skills in "real world" situations help students retain, retrieve, and use the learning in new contexts. Such assessments that make sense and have meaning for students offer extra learning opportunities to reinforce student knowledge and skills while generating data for grades.

A Safe Learning Environment. Effective teaching practices need to occur in physically and psychologically safe climates. A safe learning environment is the keystone for learning. Effective teachers create physically and emotionally safe learning environments in which students can take academic risks, make mistakes, obtain feedback, and revise their initial ideas and understandings. In these settings, students and teachers share a mutual respect and rapport. Everyone appreciates the diversity of students' backgrounds and learning styles; and teachers and students openly accept all students' contributions. In this environment, students see themselves as capable and worthy of successful achievement; and they are willing to invest the effort needed to learn.

High-quality teachers build a sense of community that vigorously supports intellectual activity and a positive attitude toward learning. Within the classroom, students help each other solve problems and build on each other's knowledge. Students understand that there is no such thing as a "dumb" question. They suggest ideas to move the group toward its goals; they advocate differing viewpoints without disrespect; they respect the individual differences in how classmates learn; and they feel pride in producing high-quality work.

A safe academic environment provides the opportunity for students to make sense of and remember the material on which they will be assessed. To create this opportunity to learn, teachers emphasize the essential content, regularly use instructional strategies that help all students learn, closely align the taught and tested curriculum, and check that students attend class regularly so they can learn. In such an environment, students meet high academic challenges with visible support from teachers and peers.

Observation, Conferencing, and Evaluation

There is a relationship between students' interest, investment, and success in schoolwork and their teachers' repertoire of techniques for student engagement (Brandt 1998; Hill and Crevola 1999; Strong et al. 1995; Wasley 1999; Wolfe 1998). In a high-quality classroom, observers see students:

- Following specific, reasonable time lines and using clear rubrics that describe a continuum of quality, from unsatisfactory to excellent, for each learning product or performance, helping students see concretely what high-quality work looks like.

- Expressing their ideas freely without teasing or embarrassment from peers or teacher.
- Continually receiving checks for understanding and getting prompt, specific feedback about their learning, affirmation for correct understanding and effort, and information tailored to help them learn from their errors.
- Receiving ongoing and varied assessments that are used diagnostically to plan instruction, to determine student mastery, and to give students prompt feedback that they can use.
- Having choices about what they study, with whom, and the manner in which they demonstrate learning.
- Having frequent occasions to work with peers.
- Having opportunities to use their learning immediately to solve a problem or to create a product or performance, increasing both their mastery and the transfer of learning to new and relevant situations.
- Connecting the curriculum to their own interests and prior learning, increasing both the personal meaning for students and the likelihood that students will remember and use what they learn.
- Showing genuine sensitivity to different cultures, language needs, gender differences, and other experiences that shape students' background knowledge (Darling-Hammond 1999; Payne 1997) and using this information to increase the curriculum's personal relevance for them.
- Analyzing and reflecting on their own work.

Educators observe high-quality teaching when they see teachers:

- Attracting students' attention and interest by using a variety of learning activities.
- Providing direct instruction for specific skills and knowledge.
- Aligning the taught and tested curriculum so that all students have opportunities to learn the content and skills on which their academic progress will be measured.

Teachers' Beliefs About Student Learning

High-quality teaching requires more than just using instructional best practices. It involves teachers' views about increasing student learning and translating these beliefs into successful teaching behaviors. These attributes are especially important for teachers working in settings with traditionally underachieving students.

First, teachers must believe in all students' ability to achieve at high levels. Teachers should genuinely like and understand their students and their families, including at-risk students, and want to work with them. These educators are committed to each student's success and work to prevent failure. Their orientation to their students, however, is professional, rather than personal. While they deeply respect and care for their students, they do not require their students' "affection" as a prerequisite for learning (Haberman 1995).

Next, teachers must believe that it is their responsibility to find ways of engaging all their students. They recognize the relationship between how they present their material and how well students will understand and apply it to new situations. As a result, these teachers make their classrooms interesting to students; and they persistently search for approaches that work best for average, gifted, disabled, troublesome, or neglected students. Effective teachers also believe that student effort, achievement, and improvement – not measured ability – determine student learning (Collopy and Green 1995; Haberman 1995).

High-quality teaching depends on teachers working collaboratively to ensure that weaker learners, with or without special labels, have rigorous curricula and classroom supports. Teacher teams cooperate inside classrooms to instruct and assess students in a variety of ways. Teachers regularly work in core teams composed of other teachers, administrators, parents, counselors, and resource educators to discuss and monitor ways to increase individual student learning and achievement.

High-quality teaching requires a focused commitment to each student's success, the professional skills to integrate the subject matter with the students' learning needs, and the ability to work collaboratively with other educators, parents, and community resources to support learning.

Assigning High-Quality Teachers to Challenging Students

Consistent placement in a high-quality teacher's classroom is the most critical factor in student learning. Unfortunately, poor and minority students, who are most dependent on their teachers for academic success, are most likely to be taught by teachers with the least content knowledge, the weakest instructional practices, and the lowest levels of licensure. For example, students in high schools in which 90% or more of the students are African American or Hispanic are more than twice as likely to be taught by teachers without certification in their subjects as are students in schools that are 90% white. Similarly, students attending secondary schools with large (75%) concentrations of poor children are 1.8 times as likely to be taught by teachers without a major in their fields as are students attending low-poverty (10%) schools (Haycock 2000). In addition, teachers in high-poverty, high-minority schools are much more likely to be inexperienced and to transfer to another school (Haycock 2000; NCES 1998). This constant turnover of teachers with little content knowledge and limited instructional repertoires can be devastating to student achievement in high-needs schools.

Teacher and teaching quality can have a large effect on the academic performance of poor, minority students. Haycock (1998) claims that a large part of the "achievement gap" between these students and others would disappear if all students had high-quality teachers. Ferguson (1998) writes that an increase of one standard deviation in the test scores of Alabama teachers who teach black children would reduce the black/white test score gap by about two-thirds. Similarly, another study (Strauss and Sawyer 1986) suggests that a 1% increase in teacher scores on the National Teacher Examination would bring about a 5% decline in the percentage of students who fail standardized competency exams.

In addition to affecting the academic success of students, the practice of assigning less-qualified teachers to more difficult classrooms also affects teacher and teaching quality. Teachers receive high prestige and other incentives for teaching Honors, Advanced Placement, and International Baccalaureate courses. These "high track" classes tend to enroll "disproportionately large numbers of White, Asian, and upper-income students" (Haycock 2000, p. 11). Better-educated teachers expect to teach the most advanced students. They also believe that their long tenure has earned them the right to work with this elite student population. This practice is so widespread and accepted that parents and students expect this consideration.

Obviously, the most academically rigorous courses require the most capable teachers. But students at lower achievement levels also need these experienced, knowledgeable educators. Students' ability to meet high academic standards and have viable life options for further education and employment depend on their having good teachers.

Increasing all students' access to high-quality teaching means challenging the traditional school culture. Rethinking our current assignment practices and restructuring professional, social, and other incentives so that high-quality teachers are assigned to the most academically needy is one way to ensure that all students have the opportunity to succeed.

Education leaders can start addressing this excellence and equity issue by avoiding concentrating beginning teachers in schools with large percentages of poor and minority children and not assigning novice teachers almost exclusively to the lowest-achieving students. The No Child Left Behind Act attempts to ensure that districts will stop hiring uncredentialed teachers. Districts also must ensure that new teachers can demonstrate mastery of the content they will teach or provide the means to help new teachers quickly learn effective instructional practices.

Districts can provide attractive incentives for qualified teachers to work with poor and minority children. For example, school districts can target highly compensated "mentor" positions to needy schools, work with local universities to recruit and develop high-quality new teacher candidates, and design professional induction programs so that new teachers can work successfully with high-challenge students (Haycock 1998). In addition, district policies that reward mature teachers with the "right" to transfer to "easier" schools deserve review within a broader context of higher achievement for all students.

Class Size

Reducing class size has become a popular approach for increasing student achievement. Several states, including California, Wisconsin, Tennessee, Nevada, North Carolina, Texas, and Virginia, have reduced class sizes in the primary grades. Eighteen other states are considering or involved in class-size reduction programs. In 1999 Congress appropriated $1.2 billion to help school districts hire new teachers to reduce primary classrooms to 18 or fewer students, with an extra $1.3 billion for this program in the year 2000. These funds are targeted to districts with high concentrations of children in poverty, as well as those with the highest overall enrollments (Stecher et al. 2001).

For decades, researchers have studied the effects of class size on student achievement. To a large extent, this recent emphasis stems from Tennessee's successful controlled experiments of class-size reduction in the primary grades. The Student/Teacher Achievement Ratio, or STAR, program involved more than 12,000 children over four years using fully qualified teachers, a standardized curriculum, and a relatively homogeneous student population (Stecher et al. 2001).

This highly controlled, longitudinal study indicates that attending a small class for three consecutive years in grades K-3 is associated with sustained academic benefits in all school subjects through grade 8, with important carryover effects. Consecutive years in small classes had the most effect on students who usually have lower performance, such as minorities or students attending inner-city schools. While demonstrating positive results, this experiment included regularly certified, experienced teachers with students assigned to certain classrooms over successive years, options not always available in other schools (Finn et al. 2001).

In addition, a review and synthesis of more than 100 class-size studies suggests that the most positive effect of small classes appears in kindergarten to third grade for mathematics and reading test scores, with results consistent across schools (Nye, Hodges, and Konstantopoulos 2000; Robinson 1990). Smaller classes can positively affect economically disadvantaged and ethnic minority student achievement (Jacobson 2001; Robinson 1990). Research also indicates that school districts that spend money to hire experienced teachers to reduce class size evidence increased test scores (Bracey 1997, p. 26). However, findings in several studies indicate that the advantages of small classes (defined as 13 to 29 pupils) in first grade may not be continued in later years (Jacobson 2001; Robinson 1990, p. 82). Regrettably, the positive effects of class size on student achievement may decrease as grade levels increase.

Even with a reduced number of students in their classes, many teachers do not change their teaching techniques to take advantage of the smaller classes. In fact, several cost-effectiveness studies of various strategies for improving student learning indicate that reducing class size has a small positive effect on achievement compared to many less costly strategies (Robinson 1990). Decreased class size is, at times, associated with an increase in the cost of additional classrooms.

The level of teaching quality in small classes may be a key variable affecting student achievement. Wisconsin's class-size initiative, SAGE (Student Achievement Guarantee in Education), started in Fall 1996 to bring the teacher/pupil ratio down to 1 to 15 in schools that serve low-income children. A study of that program found that some teaching strategies appear to be more effective than others in increasing student achievement within the smaller classes. To make the most of small class size in the early grades, effective teachers focus on basic skills when they have one-on-one contact with students, ask students to discuss and demonstrate what they know, and use a firm but nurturing approach to classroom management. Teachers in higher-achieving first-grade classrooms also tend to establish routines, set goals, and provide frequent feedback. These approaches in smaller classes were more effective than project-oriented activities, problem-solving lessons, and efforts to give students more freedom in the classroom (Jacobson 2001).

California's experience with reducing class size is instructive. That state's $1 billion class-size reduction program in grades K-3 began in Fall 1996. Students who were enrolled in first-grade classes that had been reduced from the statewide average of 30 students to a maximum of 20 students did perform slightly better on standardized tests than did students in larger classes (Stecher et al. 2001). Third-graders enrolled in smaller classes performed better on the Stanford 9 Achievement Test than did students in regular classes. These gains lasted after students advanced to fourth grade. However, the gains did not reduce the gap between poor, minority children and others. Moreover, the reduced class size did not influence teaching quality. "Classroom instruction in smaller classes was generally no different from that in larger classes; regardless of class size, teachers [covered the same content in the same amount of time and] used similar teaching strategies" (Stecher et al. 2001, p. 673).

These small achievement gains in smaller classes come at high cost. While the California teacher workforce increased by 38% in two years to accommodate the class-size initiative, the drop in teacher quality disproportionately affected urban districts already struggling with overcrowding, poverty, and language barriers (Stecher et al. 2001). Schools have seen sharp declines in new teachers' average education level, experience, and credentials.

Class size matters most in the early elementary grades, where classes of 20 or fewer students are most effective. However, small class sizes, by themselves, are not the answer to increased learning. Research does not support the expectation that just reducing the size of classes results in greater academic gains. Class-size effects vary by grade level, pupil characteristics, subject areas, teaching methods, and other variables. Thus reducing class size without simultaneously improving teacher and teaching quality appears to be both an expensive and often unproductive option.

Professional Development

Attracting and retaining high-quality teachers depends in part on providing them with support. Professional development is an important means to help teachers enhance their teaching quality and to increase their professional satisfaction. New teachers can get better, marginal teachers can improve, and successful teachers can continue to strengthen their expertise through well-designed professional development programs.

Professional development for teachers can affect student achievement. The 1996 NAEP study (Blair 2000; Wenglinsky 2000) indicated that professional development in cultural diversity, teaching students with limited English proficiency, and teaching special needs students are all linked to higher math test scores. Every extra factor for individualizing teaching for students increases their achievement.

Professional development that explicitly describes the generic act of teaching can give faculty a common language with which to discuss teaching and learning. Systematic study of learning processes results in more effective teaching behaviors used in the classroom and increases student achievement. When teachers have opportunities to develop their own understanding of learning, they become able to analyze their own instructional practices. Informed with current perspectives and strategies, they can address students' learning needs and use a variety of strategies to help all students to learn (Munro 1999).

In addition, teachers who believe that their own instructional practices have a direct effect on student learning are more likely to seek and implement new ideas to increase student achievement (Scribner 1999). Educators who are confident in their own teaching skills want to learn more about their content and expand and sharpen their pedagogical skills. They synthesize knowledge gained in professional development, formal coursework, and informal study to use in their classrooms. They continually reflect on their professional practice, asking how to best organize and present content to suit their learners' prior knowledge, special needs, and learning styles. They consider which instructional practices are working well and with which students. They ask how they might connect more effectively with less motivated and weaker students to maximize their learning.

Not all professional development is equally effective. Effective programs are ongoing, collaborative and collegial, highly connected to what teachers actually do in their classrooms (job embedded), and driven by results (Anderson 2001). In one study, researchers found that teachers who participate in professional development that is sustained and based on curriculum standards are more likely to adopt new, reform-oriented teaching practices; and their students achieve at higher levels on state mathematics achievement tests (Hirsch, Koppich, and Knapp 1998).

Professional development is most effective when it is tied closely to actual classroom practices. For example, programs that help teachers learn how to promote students' concept building through concrete, hands-on activities, meaningful applications, and simulations increase students' math and science achievement. When principals design professional development programs, they should select learning activities that address the questions, "Does this instructional behavior increase student learning?" and "Does it work for students and teachers in measurable, observable ways?" Focusing on what teachers are able to do at the end of the program points principals toward the necessary components for effective professional development.

Teachers want activities that are immediately practical and relevant. They use learning that directly connects to their own work with students, links to concrete teaching tasks, organizes around solving problems, reflects current research, and continues over time with coaching, collaboration, and conversation. In addition, teachers benefit when the presenters, themselves, model high-quality instructional practices.

Professional development that increases teaching quality is ongoing. Meeting weekly, bi-monthly, or monthly with an expert facilitator and a small group of interested colleagues gives teachers repeated opportunities to learn, practice, and master defined skills. They can try out new approaches in their classrooms and receive feedback from colleagues who observe them. Teachers can use this feedback to polish and refine their next attempts. Over time, these learning activities create change for teachers and students. Moreover, principals give critical support when they provide teachers with regular time within the contract day to collaboratively focus on ways to increase student achievement through improved instructional practices.

Professional development also promotes teachers' continual self-assessments and reflections about their techniques and the degree to which they are supporting all students' achievement. High-quality professional development helps teachers analyze their own work, determine its effect on student learning, and modify future instruction as student feedback indicates.

At least 32 states require professional development as part of teacher certification renewal. These requirements would better promote high-quality teaching if they tied their "clock hours" to regulations guiding the quality of content, the sustained nature of ongoing professional learning, and its classroom implementation and practice with collegial consultation and feedback as part of the renewal obligation (Hirsch, Koppich, and Knapp 1998).

Teacher Induction and Mentoring Programs

Teaching is the only profession without a built-in apprenticeship period, and preparation programs vary widely in the extent and quality of field experiences. Nevertheless, schools expect new teachers to do the same job as 15-year veterans. To make the job still more difficult for novices, teaching is frequently an isolating profession with little encouragement or time for sharing with peers. New teachers who have the support of induction and mentoring programs are more likely to stay in the profession and get beyond their initial concerns with classroom management to focus on student learning (Gold 1996).

Novice teachers need more than good wishes and superficial support if they are to grow as teachers and remain in the profession. "New teachers want and need a tutor who will teach them how to teach and show them what to do. . . . What they want is an induction program" (Wong 2001, pp. 46, 50). A number of districts, including Cincinnati, Columbus, and Toledo, Ohio, and Rochester, New York, have reduced the attrition rates of beginning teachers from more than 30% to less than 5% by providing an induction program with expert mentors who have release time to coach beginners in their first year (Darling-Hammond 2001).

"Induction" and "mentoring" are often used interchangeably, but they mean slightly different things. Induction is a process of systematically training and supporting new teachers, beginning before the first day of school and continuing through the first two or three years of teaching. The purposes include easing the novice's transition into teaching, improving teaching effectiveness, learning the district's culture, and increasing the retention rate for highly qualified teachers (Wong 2001).

Mentoring refers to specific behaviors in the induction process, including having mature teachers provide moral support and practical suggestions to the new professional during the first year of teaching. Mentoring may be a more informal relationship than induction is. However, both mentoring and induction help novices successfully adjust to their new profession.

Typically, induction programs last one or more years and connect novice teachers with senior teachers so that the novices become familiar with the school's norms. The senior teachers share information and provide support while they help the novices prevent and solve problems. New teachers meet with a senior teacher on a regular, frequent schedule. They discuss the "how-to's" of first-year teaching: how to compile a successful gradebook, how to manage a classroom, how to complete essential forms, how to grade student work effectively, how to complete report cards, how to conference with parents, and other first-year teacher concerns. Novice teachers may receive invitations to observe others' classrooms to note effective teaching practices and talk with the senior teacher afterward to understand the instructional decisions.

Mentoring is a more collegial, supportive relationship in which, ideally, mentors and new teachers meet regularly to instruct, inquire, and reflect on all aspects of the teaching craft, with a particular emphasis on student performance (Anderson 2001). This is a one-to-one relationship that varies greatly in structure and formality, depending on the school and the individuals involved. Mentoring is more than an orientation but usually less than a systematic program of ongoing pragmatic, collegial support.

One effective induction program that includes mentoring is the Peer Assistance and Evaluation program in the Cincinnati Public Schools. This program assigns all new teachers to consulting teachers – advanced or accomplished teachers in the same subject and grade level – who are released from classroom duties to work with up to 14 teachers (Keiffer-Barone and Ware 2001). Consulting teachers orient new hires to the district schools, assist with curriculum and content, and mentor teaching skills. They collaborate in lesson planning, team-teach, and meet monthly in seminars on important instructional and management issues. Consulting teachers also observe new teachers' classrooms and evaluate their performance according to clear and high standards. Experienced teachers who show serious instructional weaknesses also may be assigned to work with a consulting teacher.

The Newport News Public Schools (NNPS) in Virginia provide a range of induction and mentoring options to support beginning teachers. First, educators use the Pathwise Instructional Mentoring Program developed by the Educational Testing Service to provide training and assistance for novice teachers. Mentors are mature teachers with classroom expertise, trained in this mentoring model, and paid a $500 stipend each year for working closely with a novice. During the school year, the mentor and mentee conduct a series of highly structured learning activities in a cycle of planning, teaching, reflecting, and applying. As colleagues, they consider how to establish a learning environment, observe professional practice, develop an individual growth plan, practice instructional strategies, analyze student work, and reflect on teaching performance. Using rubrics that describe different levels of proficiency, new teachers can assess their current practice and look ahead to see what their skills can become. In this continuing, dynamic approach, mentors support new teachers' development as reflective practitioners who are increasingly skilled at analyzing their own practice, sharing ideas with other new teachers, and learning from more experienced colleagues.

NNPS boasts four additional mentor programs to induct new teachers into the profession and increase teacher retention. New teachers in NNPS without a Pathwise Mentor receive mentoring through a site-based mentor program in each school. Mentors in the site-based program are eligible to receive up to 45 points toward their teaching license renewal. In addition, a New Teacher Academy connects novice teachers with their assistant principals for a year of intensive support. Next, a Minority Male Mentor Program has monthly support meetings for a cadre of minority male teachers, allowing these new teachers to interact with positive role models from throughout the Newport News community. In a student population that is more than 50% minority, attracting and keeping effective male minority teachers provides constructive messages about high academic achievement. Finally, both pre-K to grade 5 and novice teachers working with NNPS elementary special education students have their own mentoring programs to induct and support them.

Many schools now use federal education funds for teacher induction and mentoring programs. The 1998 federal law designed to reduce class sizes has "wiggle room" that permits some of the money to be spent to make better teachers, rather than simply hiring more. For example, the Denver Public Schools used federal funds to experiment with a mentoring approach. They designed the Primary Lead Teacher (PLT) program to increase their teachers' skills by offering them training from colleagues with extensive experience in fostering student literacy and up-to-date knowledge of literacy research and teaching methods. PTLs work with both teachers and students in primary classrooms to demonstrate techniques for teaching literacy. They also observe and conference with teachers about enhanced instructional practice and present professional development activities to teachers. As both teachers and students have improved their skills, students' assessment scores increase (Sack 2001).

Little empirical evidence verifies the effects of different induction or mentoring programs on new teachers or their students. Mentoring, though a popular approach to support new teachers, may be more honored in its ideal than in its effect. Wong notes that "few comprehensive studies exist that have examined in depth the context, content, and consequences of mentoring" (2001, p. 50), and more direct studies are needed to determine its effect on teaching and teacher retention. He adds, "We cannot jeopardize an entire generation of new teachers with a 20-year-old process (mentoring) that has not produced any systematic results and still requires 'more direct studies'."

The literature also provides no clear answers about the degree to which induction should focus on assistance or assessment; the types of mentorships that best support new teachers' adaptation; what standards should apply to the role, the selection, and the preparation of mentors; or the time necessary for effective mentor/mentee relationships (Berry and Haselkorn 1996).

Anecdotal evidence nevertheless affirms that effective induction and mentoring can help new teachers improve their teaching quality and remain in the profession. Any effective induction or mentor program must remember that "The trick for survival in teaching is to keep idealism as a motivation, but develop a clinical realism for the day-to-day action" (Wong 2001, p. 50).

Instructional Coaching

Instructional coaching is a highly focused program of in-house professional development for educating teachers about the most recent, research-based, classroom practices in teaching, curriculum, and assessment. Coaches work *with* teachers, rather than *teach* them.

In this professional development model, an expert "coach" —
usually a former teacher with recognized skills — works with a
group of teachers in a consultation customized to teachers' and
students' specific learning needs. Coaches model classroom
teaching practices, team-teach with colleagues to demonstrate
new approaches, observe and provide specific feedback to teachers implementing the new practices, and organize teacher collaboration in evaluating student work (Guiney 2001). Coaches build
trust with teachers. Instead of "Do this!" coaches use, "Here is an
idea. Try it." Over time, teachers develop enhanced teaching
skills and are ready to lead other teachers to build similar skills.

For example, the Boston Public Schools use content coaches as
vehicles for school reform. Superintendent Thomas Payzant's
standards-based reform goal focuses on using professional development to improve instruction, placing a clear emphasis on helping teachers work together, making their work public, and ending
teacher isolation. Through weekly guidance and instructional
modeling, teachers improve their teaching quality; and students'
standardized test scores are higher at many of the schools in
which coaches have been working longest (Guiney 2001). *PLC*

Many believe that teachers' ability to create a professional
learning community is an essential part of improving teaching and
student achievement. Small, intimate, and ongoing professional
communities that create opportunities for support, encouragement, detailed study of student achievement data, and problem
solving have a positive effect on teachers' classroom practice and
student learning (Ladson-Billings and Gomez 2001).

National Teacher Certification

The National Board for Professional Teaching Standards
(NBPTS), established in 1987, sets high standards for what teachers know and do, operates a voluntary national system to assess
and certify teachers, and advances education reform. Increasingly
popular, almost 10,000 teachers received NBPTS certification in
2000, up from 1,800 in 1988-89 (Bohen 2001; Harman 2001).

Advocates state that the NBPTS certification spells out the high standards for content knowledge and pedagogy essential to enhance teaching quality. "Teachers find the certification process, especially the creation of the portfolio, a powerful and transforming professional development experience" (Bohen 2001, p. 50). The NBPTS 10-month certification process connects teaching and student learning. The portfolio-building process includes teachers videotaping and analyzing their lessons to assess the instructional effect on student learning and reflecting on how to improve both the lesson and the learning. Teachers also evaluate student data and products, learn to question their instructional decisions, and accept responsibility for student outcomes. NBPTS asserts that, as teachers document and articulate their practice, they expand and adjust their perceptions about teaching. At the same time, says the board, these teachers improve their classroom performance in ways that improve student learning (Bohen 2001).

Prominent teacher agencies give the NBPTS certification widespread recognition and support. Increasingly universities have incorporated the NBPTS standards into teacher preparation and professional accreditation programs. The American Federation of Teachers and the National Education Association have jointly published a guidebook to help teachers gain this endorsement. Other prominent organizations, such as the Carnegie Foundation for the Advancement of Teaching, Teachers College Columbia University, and the National Council for Accreditation of Teacher Education, are helping the NBPTS to meet its goals. Governors, state legislatures, and school boards help school districts provide a range of incentives for teachers to earn certification (Bohen 2001). Forty states already encourage teachers to seek NBPTS certification by offering financial reimbursements and salary supplements (Harman 2001). For example, Florida subsidizes 90% of the application fee and provides teachers who achieve certification with a 10% annual salary increase during the certificate's 10-year life (Harman 2001).

No evidence exists that National Board for Professional Teaching Standards certification correlates with measures of student achievement (Wilcox 2000). Educators can fully support clear standards, content, and pedagogy that enhance teaching and learning but might want to wait for gains in student achievement before claiming that NBPTS certification is the answer to the teacher and teaching quality issue.

High-Stakes Tests

High-stakes tests are driving the accountability movement. The No Child Left Behind legislation requires all states to begin annual standardized testing of students' reading and math skills in certain grades as well as in identified high school subjects. Until this mandate, 49 states had testing initiatives to raise schools' academic standards, and 48 states had testing programs to measure student achievement with state-adopted standards (Olson 2000).

Some argue that high-stakes tests are harming teachers' professional working environment. Many effective teachers have their favorite topics and enjoy having students learn them, regardless of whether the content will appear on high-stakes tests. Other excellent educators value students taking time to study important issues in depth and creatively. However, especially if the consequences for failing are high, students must have opportunity to learn the material on which they will be assessed. Ethically and practically, teachers must align what they teach to what the test will measure. To some extent, testing restricts teachers' professional choices about what they will teach.

To remedy low test scores, some public schools, such as those in Chicago, are requiring teachers to "implement authorized, packaged lesson plans that focus exclusively on direct instruction for every subject area" (Lederhouse 2001, p. 39). Although it is an unintended consequence, paring down what is taught to meet the narrowly assessed curriculum may reduce teachers' roles to that of technician, rather than professional creator and adapter of instruction. If decision-making ability defines a profession, limiting teachers' autonomy makes a career in public education less inviting to many intelligent educators (Lederhouse 2001).

Not all high-stakes testing programs are perceived as equally stringent. One study found that where the state standards impose high levels of external pressure, the curriculum taught to students tends to align with what is taught with the test. Where little external pressure exists, little change in teaching behavior is seen (Firestone and Mayrowetz 2000). Therefore external pressure appears to be an important factor in changing teacher behavior.

There is considerable debate on how high-stakes tests affect teaching quality. Some believe that such tests decrease the richness of teaching quality and force teachers to cover only the content of the test. Others believe that high-stakes tests focus teaching quality on a common and high-quality target. However, few studies have attempted to quantify teacher beliefs about high-stakes tests and to relate them to the use of instructional best practices. One study (Kaplan and Owings 2001) found that teachers expressed strong support for high-stakes tests where:

- Instructional best practices are used and teachers are encouraged to teach to each student's learning needs.
- Student progress is monitored closely and assessment of student work is ongoing and aligned with the standards.
- Students who are not achieving satisfactorily are given sufficient opportunity for learning.

In other words, where high-quality teaching exists, those teachers tend to support high-stakes testing.

External pressure may change what content is taught, but it is less effective in changing instructional practices. Investigators and critics agree that a persistent pattern of teaching exists in the United States that is characterized by "lectures and recitation, students using worksheets requiring simplistic answers, and too many topics covered too shallowly" (Firestone and Mayrowetz 2000, p. 735). In interviews, teachers repeatedly confess a lack of ability to change classroom instruction even in the face of external pressure from high-stakes tests (Firestone and Mayrowetz 2000).

Teachers believe they already are teaching effectively. Often they need specific feedback about their own students' performance on tests before they can reflect accurately on their instructional practices. To enhance teaching quality and to enable students to meet standards, states and localities must provide support to teachers. Part of that support involves professional development in disaggregating data to determine the underlying causes of low scores. Educators must be able to determine if their own students' poor achievement is due to curriculum misalignment, poor teaching quality, inadequate resources, or student reading problems.

Teachers benefit from reviewing their own students' test data, as well as the test data of successful students in demographically similar schools. Accurately determining why students score as they do eliminates traditional excuses for poor achievement. If principals and teachers address alignment, reading, and resource issues and student scores still do not rise, teachers must consider their own instructional practices. Teachers may have to increase their instructional repertoire to ensure that all students learn.

Finally, high-stakes testing is both a policy and a practical issue. To avoid oversimplifying this complex matter, educators must always ask if the high-stakes tests address the "right" standards. Is the content domain assessed adequately and appropriately, and are the accountability practices suitable? Teaching to inappropriate standards is an ethical issue of significant professional importance that must be brought to the public forum. Moreover, responsible educators continue to define appropriate student learning targets.

The implications for high-stakes tests and teaching quality are clear. Where instructional best practices exist, teachers tend to support such standards. Where these standards impose greater external pressure on schools, teachers tend to change their teaching behaviors.

Conclusion

What teachers know makes a difference in what students learn. Content knowledge, licensure, and certification have a demonstrated effect on how much students achieve. In addition, teaching quality, what teachers do in the classroom, also has a significant effect on what students learn.

In the past decade, policy makers have tried to reform schools by imposing increased graduation requirements, tougher standards, and high-stakes testing on students. On their own, these new requirements will not do anything to improve student achievement. Unless changes occur inside the classroom with improved teaching and learning, our students will not meet the idealistic challenge of No Child Left Behind. Quality teachers and quality teaching are the keys to success.

We know what constitutes good teaching, and we know what factors contribute to being a better teacher. If principals, superintendents, and other instructional leaders are going to meet the challenges facing them, they need to recruit high-quality teachers and support high-quality teaching in their schools.

These enhancements to teacher and teaching quality will not be achieved without cost. To not pay the price will come at an even greater cost to society

References

Anderson, P.K. "But What If . . . Supporting Leaders and Learners." *Phi Delta Kappan* 82 (June 2001): 737-39.

Archer, J. "Fla. District Signs Teachers Early." *Education Week*, 30 May 2001, p. 4. a

Archer, J. "New Roles Tap Expertise of Teachers." *Education Week*, 30 May 2001, p. 1, 16-18. b

Archer, J. "Va. School Sees Board-Certified Teachers as Key to Turnaround." *Education Week*, 30 May 2001, p. 17. c

Archer, J.; Hoff, D.J.; and Manzo, K.K. "Economic Boom Eluded Teachers, Surveys Suggest." *Education Week*, 30 May 2001, p. 10.

Associated Press. "Surveys: Teacher Salaries Don't Keep Pace With Inflation." 17 May 2001.

Ballou D., and Podgursky, M. "Reforming Teacher Training and Recruitment: A Critical Appraisal of the Recommendations of the National Commission on Teaching and America's Future." *Government Union Review* 17, no. 4 (1997): 1-53.

Ballou D., and Podgursky, M. "Teacher Training and Licensure: A Layman's Guide." In *Better Teachers, Better Schools*, edited by M. Kanstoroom and C.E. Finn Jr. Washington, D.C.: Thomas Fordham Foundation, 1999.

Basinger, J. "Colleges Widen Alternative Routes to Teacher Certification." *Chronicle of Higher Education*, 14 January 2000, pp. A18-A19.

Berry, B. "No Shortcuts to Preparing Good Teachers." *Educational Leadership* 58 (May 2001): 32-36.

Berry, B., and Haselkorn, D. *Transforming Teacher Recruitment, Selection, and Induction: Capturing Both the Frame and the Picture for Reform and Professionalism.* New York: National Commission for Teaching and America's Future, Teachers College, Columbia University, 1996.

Blair, J. "ETS Study Links Effective Teaching Methods to Test-Score Gains." *Education Week*, 25 October 2000, pp. 24-25.

Blair, J. "In Ky., Master Teachers Find They Can't Go Home Again." *Education Week*, 30 May 2001, p. 19. a

Blair, J. "Iowa Approves Performance Pay for Its Teachers." *Education Week*, 16 May 2001, pp. 1, 24-25. b

Blair, J. "New Accreditor Gaining Toehold in Teacher Ed." *Education Week*, 23 May 2001, pp. 1, 12-13. c

Bohen, D.B. "Strengthening Teaching Through National Certification." *Educational Leadership* 58 (June 2001): 50-53.

Bracey, G. *Setting the Record Straight.* Alexandria, Va.: Association for Supervision and Curriculum Development, 1997.

Brandt, R. *Powerful Learning*. Alexandria, Va.: Association for Supervision and Curriculum Development, 1998.

Chase, B. "For Every Child, a Qualified Teacher." *Thinking K-16* 4 (Spring 2000): 14.

Cobb, R.B., et al. "An Examination of Colorado's Teacher Licensure Testing." *Journal of Educational Research* 92 (January/February 1999):167-75.

Coleman, J.S.; Campbell, E.Q.; Hobson, C.J.; McPartland, J.; Mood, A.M.; Weinfeld, F.D.; and York, R.L. *Equality of Educational Opportunity*. Washington, D.C.: U.S. Government Printing Office, 1966.

Collopy, R.B., and Green, T. "Using Motivational Theory with At-Risk Children." *Educational Leadership* 53 (September 1995): 37-40.

Danielson, C. *Enhancing Professional Practice: A Framework for Teaching*. Alexandria, Va.: Association for Supervision and Curriculum Development, 1996.

Darling-Hammond, L. *Doing What Matters Most: Investing in Quality Teaching*. New York: National Commission on Teaching and America's Future, 1997.

Darling-Hammond, L. "Educating Teachers for the Next Century: Rethinking Practice and Policy." In *The Education of Teachers: Ninety-Eighth Yearbook of the National Society for the Study of Education*. Chicago: University of Chicago Press, 1999.

Darling-Hammond, L. "Teacher Quality and Student Achievement: A Review of State Policy Evidence." *Education Policy Analysis Archives*, 1 January 2000. www.epaa.asu.edu/epaa/v8n1

Darling-Hammond, L. "The Challenge of Staffing Our Schools." *Educational Leadership* 58 (June 2001): 12-17.

Feiman-Nemser, S., and Parker, M.B. *Making Subject Matter Part of the Conversation or Helping Beginning Teachers Learn to Teach.* East Lansing, Mich.: National Center for Research on Teacher Education, 1990.

Ferguson, R.F. "Paying for Public Education: New Evidence on How and Why Money Matters." *Harvard Journal on Legislation* 28 (Summer 1991): 465-98.

Ferguson, R.F. "Can Schools Narrow the Black-White Test Score Gap?" In *The Black-White Test Score Gap,* edited by C. Jencks and M. Phillips. Washington D.C.: Brookings Institution, 1998.

Fideler, E., and Haselkorn, D. *Learning the Ropes: Urban Teacher Induction Programs and Practices in the United States.* Belmont, Mass.: Recruiting New Teachers, 1999.

Finn, C.E., Jr., and Madigan, K. "Removing the Barriers for Teacher Candidates." *Educational Leadership* 58 (June 2001)*:* 29-31, 36.

Finn, J.D.; Gerber, S.B.; Achilles, C.M.; and Boyd-Zaharias, J. "The Enduring Effects of Small Classes." *Teachers College Record* 103 (2001): 145-83.

Firestone, W.A., and Mayrowetz, D. *Rethinking "High Stakes": Lessons from the U.S. and England and Wales.* New York: Teachers College Press, 2000.

Fowler, R.C. "What Did the Massachusetts Teacher Tests Say About American Education?" *Phi Delta Kappan* 82 (June 2001): 773-80.

Gold, Y. "Beginning Teacher Support: Attrition, Mentoring, and Induction." In *Handbook of Research in Teacher Education.* New York: Macmillan, 1996.

Goldhaber, D.D., and Brewer, D.J. "Teacher Licensing and Student Achievement." In *Better Teachers, Better Schools*, edited by M. Kanstoroom and C.E. Finn Jr. Washington, D.C.: Thomas Fordham Foundation, 1999.

Goodnough, A. "Shortage Ends as City Lures New Teachers." *New York Times*, 23 August 2002, pp. 1-3.

Grissmer, D. "Factors in Teacher Supply and Demand." In *Teachers: Supply and Demand in an Age of Rising Standards.* Amherst, Mass.: National Evaluation Systems, 2000.

Guiney, E. "Coaching Isn't Just for Athletes: The Role of Teacher Leaders." *Phi Delta Kappan* 82 (June 2001): 740-43.

Guyton, E., and Farokhi, E. "Relationships Among Academic Performance, Basic Skills, and Subject Matter Knowledge and Teaching Skills of Teacher Education Graduates." *Journal of Teacher Education* 38, no. 5 (1987): 37-42.

Haberman, M. "Selecting 'Star' Teachers for Children and Youth in Urban Poverty." *Phi Delta Kappan* 76 (June 1995): 777-81.

Harman, A.E. "A Wider Role for the National Board." *Educational Leadership* 58 (June 2001): 54-55.

Haycock, K. "Good Teaching Matters... A Lot." *Thinking K-16* 3 (Summer 1998): 3-14.

Haycock, K. "No More Settling for Less." *Thinking K-16* 4 (Spring 2000): 3-8, 10-12.

Haycock, K.; Jerald, C.; and Huang, S. " Closing the Gap: Done in a Decade." *Thinking K-16* 5 (Spring 2001): 3-22.

Hayward, E. "Judge Clears Way for Math Teacher Tests." *Boston Herald,* 8 May 2001. www.bostonhera...ws/local_regional/math05082001.htm

Hill, P.W., and Crevola, C.A. "The Role of Standards in Educational Reform for the 21st Century." In *Preparing Our Schools for the 21st Century*, ASCD 1999 Yearbook, edited by D.D. Marsh. Alexandria, Va.: Association for Supervision and Curriculum Development, 1999.

Hirsch, E.; Koppich, J.E.; and Knapp, M.S. *What States Are Doing to Improve the Quality of Teaching. A Brief Review of Current Patterns and Trends*. Seattle: Center for the Study of Teaching and Policy, December 1998.

Ingersoll, R.M. "The Realities of Out-of-Field Teaching." *Educational Leadership* 58 (June 2001): 42-45.

Ingersoll, R.M. "The Teacher Shortage: A Case of Wrong Diagnosis and Wrong Perception." *NASSP Bulletin* 86 (July 2002): 16-31.

Jacobson, L. "Wis. Class-Size Study Yields Advice On Teachers' Methods." *Education Week*, 24 January 2001, p. 15.

Jelmberg, J.R. "College-Based Teacher Education Versus State-Sponsored Alternative Programs." *Journal of Teacher Education* 47, no. 1 (1996): 60-66.

Jordan, H.R.; Mendro, R.L.; and Weerasinghe, D. "Teacher Effects on Longitudinal Student Achievement." Paper presented at the CREATE Annual Meeting, Indianapolis, Ind., July 1997.

Jorgenson, O. "Supporting a Diverse Teacher Corps." *Educational Leadership* 58 (June 2001): 64-67.

Kain, J.F., and Singleton, K. "Equality of Educational Opportunity Revisited." *New England Economic Review* (May/June 1996): 87-114.

Kanstoroom, M., and Finn, C.E., Jr., eds. *Better Teachers, Better Schools*. Washington, D.C.: Thomas B. Fordham Foundation, 1999.

Kaplan, L.S., and Owings, W.A. "How Principals Can Help Teachers With High-Stakes Testing: One Survey's Findings with National Implications." *NASSP Bulletin* 85 (February 2001): 15-23.

Keiffer-Barone, S., and Ware, K. "Growing Great Teachers in Cincinnati." *Educational Leadership* 58 (June 2001): 56-59.

Knapp, M.S.; Shields, P.M.; and Turnbull, B.J. "Academic Challenge in High-Poverty Classrooms." *Phi Delta Kappan* 76 (June 1995): 770-76.

Ladson-Billings, G., and Gomez, M.L. "Just Showing Up: Supporting Early Literacy Through Teachers' Professional Communities." *Phi Delta Kappan* 82 (May 2001): 675-80.

Lederhouse, J.N. "Show Me the Power." *Education Week*, 13 June 2001, pp. 36, 39.

Levinson, A. "How to Put Our Teachers to the Test." *The Daily Press*, 22 July 2001, pp. I1, I3.

Madaus, G., and Pullin, D. "Teacher Certification Tests: What Do They Tell Us?" *Phi Delta Kappan* 69 (September 1987): 31-38.

Markley, M. "Area School Districts Finding New Ways to Attract Teachers." *Houston Chronicle*, 30 April 2001. http://www.chron.com/cs/CDA/story.hts/metropolitan/893228

Minner, S. "Our Own Worst Enemy: Why Are We So Silent on the Issue That Matters Most?" *Education Week*, 30 May 2001, p. 33.

Mitchell, R., and Barth, P. "How Teacher Licensing Tests Fall Short." *Thinking K-16* 3 (Spring 1999): 3-21.

Monk, D.H. "Subject Matter Preparation of Secondary Mathematics and Science Teachers and Student Achievement." *Economics of Education Review* 13, no. 2 (1994):125-45.

Monk, D.H., and King, J.A. "Multi-level Teacher Resource Effects in Pupil Performance in Secondary Mathematics and Science: The Case of Teacher Subject Matter Preparation." In *Choices and Consequences: Contemporary Policy Issues in Education*, edited by R.G. Ehrenberg. Ithaca, N.Y.: ILR Press, 1994.

Munro, J. "Learning More About Learning Improves Teacher Effectiveness." *School Effectiveness and School Improvement* 10 (June 1999): 151-71.

National Center for Educational Statistics (NCES). *Digest of Education Statistics*. Washington, D.C.: U.S. Department of Education, 1998.

National Commission on Teaching and America's Future. *What Matters Most: Teaching for America's Future*. New York, 1996.

National Council for Accrediting of Teacher Education (NCATE). "NCATE 2000: Performance-Based Accreditation." In *NCATE: Making a Difference*. Washington, D.C., September 2000.

Ness, M. "Lessons of a First-Year Teacher." *Phi Delta Kappan* 82 (June 2001) : 700-701.

Nye, B.; Hodges, L.V.; and Konstantopoulos, S. "The Effects of Small Class Sizes on Academic Achievement: The Results of the Tennessee Class Size Experiment." *American Educational Research Journal* 37 (Spring 2000): 123-51.

Okamoto, L. "Teacher-Pay Revision Begins: Lack of Enthusiasm from Educators Is Called a Bad Sign." *Des Moines Register*, 24 May 2001. www.dmregiste...ews/stories/c4780934/14782193.html

Olson, L. "Worries of a Standards 'Backlash' Grow." *Education Week,* 5 April 2000, pp. 1, 12-13.

Payne, R. *Learning Structures Inside the Head*. Baytown, Tex.: RFT, 1997.

Reeves, D.B. "Standards Are Not Enough: Essential Transformations for School Success." *NASSP Bulletin* 84 (December 2000): 5-13.

Reid, K.S. "Prep-School Program Opens Doors for Minority Teachers." *Education Week*, 8 August 2001, pp. 6-7.

Resta, V.; Huling, L.; and Rainwater, N. "Preparing Second Career Teachers." *Educational Leadership* 58 (June 2001): 60-63.

Robinson, G.E. "Synthesis of Research on the Effects of Class Size." *Educational Leadership* 47 (April 1990): 80-90.

Ross, F. "Helping Immigrants Become Teachers." *Educational Leadership* 58 (June 2001): 68-71.

Sack, J.L. "Subtraction by Addition: Some Districts Use Class-Size Money on Teacher-Mentors." *Education Week*, 13 June 2001, pp. 1, 25.

Sanders, W.L., and Rivers, J.C. *Cumulative and Residual Effects of Teachers on Future Student Academic Achievement*. Knoxville: University of Tennessee, Tennessee Value Added Assessment System, November 1996.

Scribner, J.P. "Teacher Efficacy and Teacher Professional Learning: Implications for School Leaders." *Journal of School Leadership* 9 (May 1999): 209-34.

Silberman, T. "Bill Seeks Flexibility in Testing Teachers." Charlotte, N.C., *News Observer*, 16 May 2001. www.newsobserv...news/nc/Story/437111p-428738c.html. a

Silberman, T. "Preparing 'Instant' Teachers." Charlotte, N.C., *News Observer*, 31 July 2001. www.newsobserv...nt/News/Story/805625p.803731c.html. b

Sprenger, M. *Learning and Memory: The Brain in Action.* Alexandria, Va.: Association for Supervision and Curriculum Development, 1999.

Stecher, B.; Bohrnstedt, G.; Kirst, M.; McRobbie, J.; and Williams, T. "Class-Size Reduction in California: A Story of Hope, Promise, and Unintended Consequences." *Phi Delta Kappan* 82 (June 2001)*:* 670-74.

Strauss, R.P., and Sawyer, E.A. "Some New Evidence on Teacher and Student Competencies." *Economics of Education Review* 5, no. 1 (1986): 41-48.

Strong, R.; Silver, H.F.; and Robinson, A. "What Do Students Want (And What Really Motivates Them?)." *Educational Leadership* 53 (September 1995): 8-12.

Tell, C. "Making Room for Alternative Routes." *Educational Leadership* 58 (June 2001): 38-41.

U.S. Department of Education. *Predicting the Need for Newly Hired Teachers in the United States, 2000-2009.* Washington, D.C., 2000.

Vaishnav, A. "Judge Gives State OK to Test Some Teachers." *Boston Globe*, 8 May 2001, p. 3. www.boston.com/dailyglobe2/...te_OK_to_test_some_teachers+.shtml

Viadero, D. "Researcher: Teacher Signing Bonuses Miss Mark in Massachusetts." *Education Week*, 21 February 2001, p. 13. www.edweek.org/ew/ewstory.cfm?slug=23bonus.h20

Wasley, P. "Teaching Worth Celebrating." *Educational Leadership* 56 (May 1999): 8-13.

Wenglinsky, H. *How Teaching Matters: Bringing the Classroom Back into Discussions of Teacher Quality.* Policy Information Center Report. Princeton, N.J.: Milken Family Foundation, Educational Testing Service, October 2000.

Wilcox, D.D. "The National Board for Professional Teaching Standards: Can It Live Up to Its Promise?" In *Better Teachers, Better Schools*, edited by M. Kanstoroom and C.E. Finn Jr. Washington, D.C.: Thomas Fordham Foundation, 2000.

Wise, A.E. "Standards or No Standards? Teacher Quality in the 21st Century." *NCATE Newsbriefs*, 27 June 2001, p. 3. www.ncate.org/newsbrfs/reforminaction.htm

Wolfe, P. "Revisiting Effective Teaching." *Educational Leadership* 56 (November 1998): 61-64.

Wong, H.K. "Mentoring Can't Do It All." *Education Week*, 8 August 2001, pp. 46, 50.

CONTEXTUAL TEACHING and LEARNING:
A Primer for Effective Instruction

Susan Sears

University researcher and practitioner Susan Sears presents a guide to reforming teaching and teacher education. This book provides an overview of how contextual teaching and learning, or CTL, can change classroom practice and teacher education programs. Using a fictional case study approach, Sears illustrates how CTL can result in teacher education reform in both a large state university and a smaller regional university.

Researchers studied four teacher education programs that were peer-nominated as exemplars of successful contextual teaching and learning. Sears drew on these studies to portray teacher education reform in institutions and programs with diverse missions and varied demands.

127pp Trade paperback. $14.95 (PDK members, $11.95)

To Order: 1-800-766-1156
A processing charge is added to all orders.

Tutor Quest:
Finding Effective Education for Children and Adults

Edward E. Gordon

*T*utor Quest is a practical handbook for individuals looking for learning assistance, whether for themselves or their children. Not only does Edward Gordon provide expert background information on tutoring, but he also includes a handy checklist to make evaluating the tutoring market easier and more effective. Included in the volume are the National Better Business Bureau Trade Practice Standards and Professional Guidelines for Educational Tutoring.

School administrators and teachers also will find this guide especially valuable in light of the No Child Left Behind legislation, when extra assistance is needed to help struggling learners in school.

127pp Trade paperback. $10.95 (PDK members, $8.95)

To Order: 1-800-766-1156
A processing charge is added to all orders.

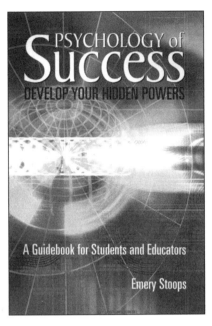

Psychology of Success:
DEVELOP YOUR HIDDEN POWERS

Emery Stoops

*P**sychology of Success* was first published in 1983, when Emery Stoops was a youthful 80 years old. An educator throughout his life — teacher, counselor, assistant principal, principal, superintendent, and college professor — Emery had embarked on a new career in the insurance industry after he was forced to retire from academe at age 65. But he did not forget his roots as a teacher.

Shortly before his 99th birthday in December 2001, Emery, still vigorous and still piling up successes, presented a revised manuscript, which we are pleased to publish in this new edition.

Emery Stoops has helped many people to discover their own psychology of success. Here is his guide to help you develop your hidden powers.

115pp Trade paperback. $14.95 (PDK members, $11.95)

To Order: 1-800-766-1156
A processing charge is added to all orders.

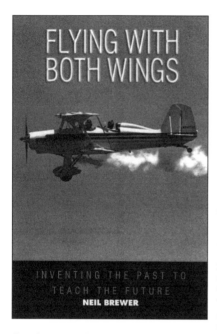

FLYING WITH BOTH WINGS:
INVENTING THE PAST TO TEACH THE FUTURE

NEIL BREWER

As social studies teacher Neil Brewer tells it, in the spring of 1993 his imagination went wild. That was when he invented his alter ego, Harmon Bidwell, a 100-year-old world traveler and adventurer who has been bringing social studies (and several other subjects) to life for elementary and middle school students across Indiana. Brewer's main instructional vehicle is a series of letters, Harmon's Letters. Through these letters, students learn about Harmon's long life and adventures, all of which teach a variety of lessons, from geography to mathematics, in a refreshing and engaging manner.

The Harmon project is innovative teaching at its best. *Flying with Both Wings* is the inspiring story of Neil Brewer's creation and the effect the Harmon Bidwell project has had on students. Most important, Brewer's account can serve to inspire other teachers to seek new and different ways to help children learn.

135pp Trade paperback. $17.95 (PDK members, $13.95)

To Order: 1-800-766-1156
A processing charge is added to all orders.